FOOTPRINTS *IN THE* ASH

JOHN MORRIS

STEVEN A. AUSTIN

FOOTPRINTS IN THE ASH

Dedicated to:
Dalta, Chara, Tim, and Beth
&
Brenda, Joel, and Daniel

Master Books

First Printing: August 2003
Second Printing: March 2005

Managing Editor: Beth Wiles
Assistant Editor: Debbie Brooks

Cover design by Left Coast Design, Portland, Oregon
Interior design by Brent Spurlock

ISBN: 0-89051-400-3
Library of Congress Catalog Card Number:
2003106349

Printed in the United States of America

Please visit our websites for other great titles:
www.masterbooks.net
www.icr.org

Contents

Introduction 8

Mount St. Helens Erupts 18

Total Devastation 38

Geologic Deposits 48

Landforms 68

Deposits in Spirit Lake 78

Rapid Fossilization 90

Rapid Revegetation 104

Evidences for Catastrophism
at Mount St. Helens 110

A Greater Significance 118

On May 18, 1980, the volcanic eruption of Mount St. Helens shocked the world with its display of unbridled explosive power. The eruption that day fundamentally challenged our way of thinking about geologic events, especially events of the past.

In contrast to most volcanic eruptions, Mount St. Helens was well studied. It had been threatening to erupt for decades and, for six weeks prior to the main eruption, it was obviously building up for a major episode. Geologists from many countries gathered at Mount St. Helens to witness the eruption and the processes it spawned. Direct observation, aerial photos, satellite images, seismographs, laser-survey devices, and even radar readouts allowed geologists to piece together, in extraordinary detail, what happened that day at the volcano.

Of great interest was the realization that the results of the Mount St. Helens eruption that *were* observed were similar to results of past processes that were *not* observed. No geologist can go back in time to observe the past, but we can observe present processes. By comparing the results of the present processes with those of past processes, we can come to some conclusions about the nature of those unknown events of the past.

Ever since the late 1700s, geologists have been accustomed to thinking about the past in terms of uniformity of processes and process rates. Their basic assumption is that things in the past occurred much the same as they occur in the present. All geologists are taught to think that "the present is the key to the past" — that only those things which are possible today have gone on in the past and that present processes, operating at essentially their present rates, scales and intensities, have accounted for all that we observe.

However, during the decade before the 1980 eruption, geologists began to express their dissatisfaction with strict uniformitarian thinking. They had noticed in the geologic record that events of the past produced rock units, fossil beds, and erosional remnants far different from the kinds

very different from the present. These scientists believed that there had been an episode of supernatural creation during the six days of the creation week mentioned in Genesis 1.

Present processes are not creative processes and thus those creation events were accomplished by different, non-uniform processes. Likewise, not long after creation, the world had been restructured by a global cataclysm in the days of Noah. Floods today achieve much geologic work, but this dynamic, world-wide hydraulic and tectonic event accomplished unimaginable amounts of geologic work in a short period of time. This work included continental tectonics, area-wide volcanism, extremely large hurricanes, and similar events. It involved large-scale erosion, deposition, and fossilization. In short, that flood would have left its mark all over the globe. No place on planet Earth escaped those great waters.

Determining the nature of the past catastrophic processes that occurred in Noah's flood has always been difficult. Such a global cataclysm is so far outside of our

Lava fountain of the Pu'u'O'o cinder & spatter cone on Kilauea Volcano Hawaii (Photo by J.D. Griggs)

of things produced today. Geologists also began to entertain the notion that episodic catastrophes had done more to shape the earth than did long periods of uniformity.

Leading the way in this revolution in geologic thinking were biblical catastrophists, those who believed that the past was at times

experience that it is hard even to imagine what it would have been like. What would be the end products of devastation on such a massive scale? Thankfully we will never again have to experience such a cataclysm. However, every now and then an event occurs in the present that expands our imagination and helps us

Volcanic eruptions bring to the surface much material formerly deep within the earth. Surprising amounts of water and gas accompany the magma to the surface. Dissolved, superhot water within magma makes for explosive eruptions on the continents and the ocean floors. (Photo by C. Heliker)

understand what the great flood of Noah's day may have been like. The eruption of Mount St. Helens did just that.

Other volcanoes have erupted in recent history and were well studied. Likewise, tsunamis have devastated coastlines. Huge earthquakes have wrought great havoc. Hurricanes have inundated coastlines, eroding and depositing sediments. None of these, however, could compare with Mount St. Helens in its variety of processes, or as a teaching tool to the earth scientist. Using it as an analogy, we can more accurately infer the nature of the processes involved in the Great Flood.

Compared to other historic volcanic eruptions, Mount St. Helens was rather small to average. Some idea of the colossal size of some ancient volcanic eruptions is shown in Figure 1. The last big explosion at Yellowstone, for example, was over 2,000 times the explosive power of Mount St. Helens.

Some may object to the use of Mount St. Helens as an analogy for Noah's flood. Mount St. Helens was a volcanic event; Noah's flood was a hydraulic event. Thus some might claim that the two could hardly be comparable.

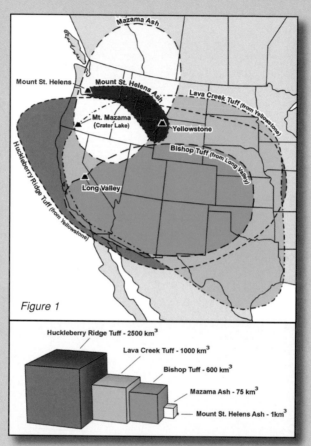

Figure 1

When the nature of both is fully understood, however, the analogy becomes quite apparent. The Great Flood, as described in the Bible, primarily involved water; but the processes God used to bring about that event were predominately volcanic and tectonic. God tells us that, "In the six hundredth year of Noah's life, in the second month, the seventeenth day of the month, the same day were all the fountains of the great deep broken up, and the windows of heaven were opened. And the rain was upon the earth forty days and forty nights" (Genesis 7:11, 12).

Evidently, the initial cause of the Flood was the breaking open of the fountains of the great deep. The "deep" in Scripture refers to the ocean, thus the "great deep" would be the deep ocean. The "fountains" appear to be a reference to ocean bottom volcanoes erupting suddenly. On that one particular day, all the fountains of the great deep were broken open. Their remains are found today all over the world. This breaking open of the earth's crust was timed on God's cue, using natural processes operating within His providential care.

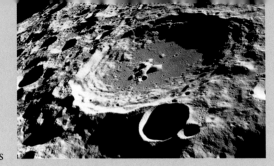

Genesis 7:11 indicates that the main power source for the Flood was internal tectonics within the earth. However, this does not disallow an external trigger event. Many Flood geologists have begun to speculate that perhaps at that moment the earth was passing through an asteroid belt or was otherwise being bombarded by meteorites. The Moon, Mars, and Venus are pockmarked with such impacts. Such a swarm could hardly have missed the Earth. The craters were mostly obliterated by the ensuing Flood waters, but remains of many large craters can still be seen, especially from satellites high above.

The word "fountains" no doubt includes volcanic events, which were spewing out not only lavas but also subterranean waters and chemicals and bringing them all to the surface. Today we know that the interior of Earth is comprised of rock that contains much water between its mineral grains — water that has never before been on the surface of the Earth. Without a doubt, much new water was added to the surface of the Earth during the Flood by these fountains.

Furthermore, we know what happens today when a volcano erupts at the bottom of the ocean. The movement of the volcano imparts energy to the surrounding water. Water is incompressible and therefore transfers that energy laterally as a giant sea wave that moves at several hundred miles per hour. If the energy wave passes beneath your boat while in deep water, you might not even notice anything unusual. However, when the water depth is shallow, the energy picks up

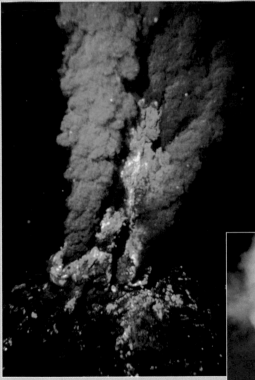

Remnants of the "fountains of the great deep" may be observed today as "black smokers" on the ocean floor. Superheated brines, containing abundant dissolved chemicals, boil the water above as they gush forth into the deep ocean.

Old Faithful is fed by an underground piping system reminiscent of pre-flood conditions.

New volcanoes sometimes erupt beneath the sea.

the water into a big wall of water that slams into the shoreline at great speed. This ocean wave is known as a tsunami or colloquially as a "tidal wave." Devastation from an individual tsunami today can be enormous. We find it hard to imagine what happened when "all the fountains of the great deep" broke open on the same day producing tsunamis that raced around the earth from every direction colliding with the continents and colliding with each other. The Flood was much more cataclysmic than we typically imagine.

The lava from these eruptions builds new islands.

Those undersea volcanic eruptions would have heated the water surrounding the underwater vent, perhaps even boiling the water above. This would have sent huge steam plumes rising into the atmosphere, where they condensed and fell as rain. The Bible says that "the windows of heaven were opened," and it must have seemed like a dam in the heavens had broken.

This is a reminder of the many volcanoes that erupted during Noah's flood.
(All photos on page by J.D. Griggs)

The Bible seems to hint that there was a great deal more water in the atmosphere before the Flood than there is now, but we know of no way that excessively large volumes of water could have been stored there. Enough moisture existed in the atmosphere to cause quite a bit of rain, but the water source had to be continually replenished by waters rising up into the atmosphere from the "fountains" below. This replenishment allowed it to rain a special rain for forty days and forty nights, but, according to the biblical account, rain continued for many days. "The fountains also of the deep and the windows of heaven were stopped, and the rain from heaven was restrained; and the waters returned from off the earth continually: and after the end of the hundred and fifty days [not just forty days] the waters were abated" (Genesis 8:2, 3). That water must have come from evaporated sea water.

Thus, we see that much of the devastation due to Noah's flood was volcanic and tectonic in nature, pointing us right back to Mount St. Helens as an analogy.

As surprising as it may seem, most of the damage done at Mount St. Helens during the 1980 eruption and its sequels was water related. To be sure, a great deal of volcanic devastation occurred, but most of the damage was done as the glaciers on the mountain's peak melted and descended catastrophically to the plains below. As that melted ice cascaded down the mountain, it removed trees, boulders, and animals. It eroded canyons and uprooted the forest. In short, it ravaged the entire area. One mudflow followed another until a series of pancake-like layers of mud and rock had been deposited in the lowlands and in the drainage basin below. These dynamic water processes added to avalanche and air-fall

Creationists speculate that great oceanic volcanoes during the Great Flood must have heated the ocean water above on a regional scale, resulting in monster hurricanes. Computer models can simulate what would happen today if the temperature in the Gulf of Mexico increased 20°F (10°C) from what it is today. The result would be a "hypercane" with an area-wide rainfall of 10 inches per hour (25 cm). The Great Flood would have been even more devastating than these hypercanes.

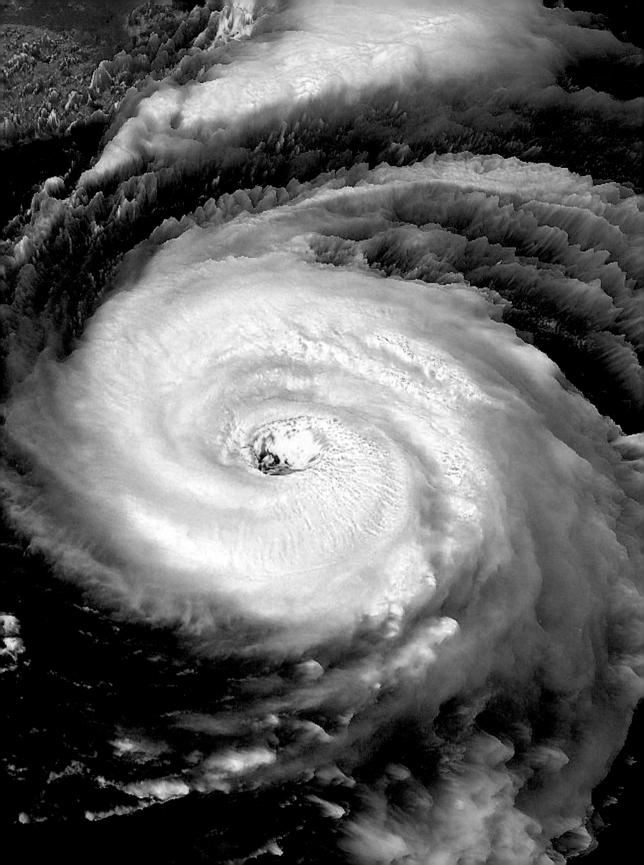

deposits which together totaled up to 600 feet (180 meters) of stratified sediments, containing dead plants and animals — some of which are now fossilizing. In a very short period of time, widespread and thorough devastation reworked a vast area.

A lake on the mountain's north flank was severely affected by the avalanching debris. By late afternoon of May 18, 1980, over one million trees floated on the lake's surface; and in the following months as those trees decayed and became waterlogged, a thick layer of peat was deposited on the lake bottom. Other mudflows and avalanches eroded huge canyons and changed the topography of the affected area.

Thus, much of the flood of Noah's day was volcanic and tectonic in nature, and much of the Mount St. Helens eruption involved water-related processes. We are justified in using Mount St. Helens as an analogue for the great flood of Noah's day.

When it was over, processes at Mount St. Helens accomplished the same sort of geologic work that biblical creationists usually attribute to the Great Flood, although on a much smaller scale and at a lower intensity. From the eruption of Mount St. Helens, which we did observe, we learned many lessons which help us understand Noah's flood, which we did not observe.

Worldwide rainfall means worldwide erosion and regional deposition of sediments. These processes would be operating at catastrophic rates, scales, and intensities far different from the kinds of processes that we observe today. According to the Bible, ". . . the world that then was (i.e. before the Flood), being overflowed with water, perished" (2 Peter 3:6). The world we live in today is the flooded, destroyed remnant of the once "very good" (Genesis 1:31) created Earth.

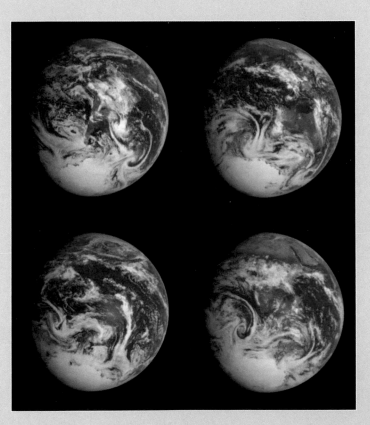

PRE-ERUPTION BEAUTY

Mount St. Helens rightly deserved its pre-eruption reputation as a sportsman's paradise with beautiful Spirit Lake on its north flank teaming with fish and fowl. Lush timberlands surrounded it on all sides, and a permanent ice cap displayed its frozen wonders all year. Considered the jewel of the Northwest, the mountain beckoned climbers and campers. Despite its beauty, geologists knew that it was alive and menacing.

Numerous streams flowed from the mountain slopes fed by abundant rain and snowfall. Campgrounds and lodges provided easy access to its attractions, and visitors flocked to the area even though geologists knew that it was unstable. In anticipation of the suspected eruption, scientific instruments and survey markers had been placed in strategic locations to observe and record any activity. Never has an eruption and its aftermath been as intensely studied as that of Mount St. Helens on May 18, 1980.

Microearthquakes between March and May 1980 indicated that magma was being injected from six-mile depths into the north flank of the mountain. On the north slope, a prominent 400-foot-high bulge (120 meters) developed by the middle of May 1980 from the magma injected beneath. Geologists grew very concerned about the water pressure within the magma. Would the eruption that followed be a steam explosion driven by 1700° F (900° C) water from the magma? Soon water pressure would reach a critical threshold, but when would effects be seen and what exactly would happen? Scientists gathered from around the world to learn all they could from the pending eruption. They were not disappointed.

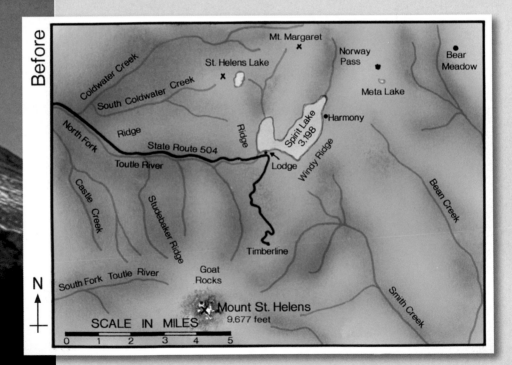

Before (May 17, 1980)

Mount St. Helens had a conical form with the swelling dome of rocks (Goat Rocks) on its north slope. Spirit Lake drained westward into the North Fork of the Toutle River which had a well integrated drainage pattern north of the volcano. Coldwater Creek and Castle Creek had no lakes. To view configurations during and following the main eruption, see maps on pages 35 and 53.

Geophysical studies of the mountain revealed that pressures building deep under the mountain were forcing molten magma toward the surface through natural passageways employed by previous eruptions. Several major eruptions had occurred within the past two thousand years each leaving a record of hardened lava and/or a coating of ash. An eruption in 1857 had been witnessed by outsiders. Native Americans told stories of earlier eruptions. All of these were just harbingers of the time bomb ticking inside.

Minor eruptions began to occur in March 1980, and continued almost daily through mid-April. Then the mountain quieted, masking the inferno within. Meanwhile, the magma continued to intrude from below, causing the mountain to expand like a balloon. For the six weeks prior to the main eruption on May 18, the mountain's north side bulged between 5 and 50 feet (2 and 15 meters) each day creating an extremely unstable slope. More than 3,000 earthquakes greater than Richter 2.5 occurred between March 20 and May 17. Government agencies ordered an evacuation of the entire area. Most left willingly, some stayed, and some sneaked back in. Of those who returned, few survived.

At 8:32 a.m. on May 18, a tremor shook the mountain, causing the over-steepened and bulging north side to slide away. Just as a soft drink bottle, in which shaking has produced excess internal pressure, "erupts" when the lid is removed, so Mount St. Helens erupted when its "lid" slid away. The eruption, when it came, blew out that weakened north side.

EVENTS AT MOUNT ST. HELENS VOLCANO

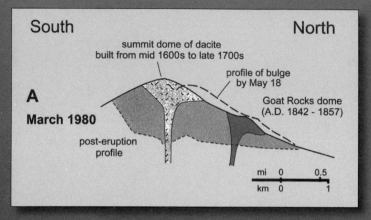

South   **North**

summit dome of dacite
built from mid 1600s to late 1700s

profile of bulge
by May 18

A

March 1980

Goat Rocks dome
(A.D. 1842 - 1857)

post-eruption
profile

mi   0   0.5
km   0   1

A. The profile of the mountain prior to the 1980 eruption shows the bulge beginning to develop on the volcano's north slope in March, April, and May 1980. Earlier eruptions produced the dacite summit dome (mid 1600s to late 1700s) and the dacite Goat Rocks Dome (1842-1857) on the north slope. The summit elevation before the 1980 eruption is 9,677 feet (2,950 meters).

B. Magma rising within the mountain is trapped by the overlying summit dome and forms the 160-million-cubic-yard (110-million-cubic-meter) cryptodome. The intrusion of the cryptodome bulges the north slope upward (450-foot elevation increase) and northward (creating a summit graben). Pressure and temperature within the mountain continue to rise. Small phreatic eruptions occur at the summit.

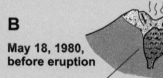

graben

B

**May 18, 1980,
before eruption**

shallow intrusion of magma produces
"cryptodome" and bulging of north slope
(March 20 - May 18, 1980)

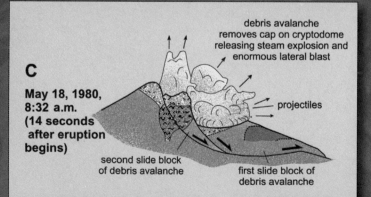

debris avalanche
removes cap on cryptodome
releasing steam explosion and
enormous lateral blast

C

**May 18, 1980,
8:32 a.m.
(14 seconds
after eruption
begins)**

projectiles

second slide block
of debris avalanche

first slide block of
debris avalanche

C. At 8:32 a.m. on May 18, 1980, a Richter magnitude 5.1 earthquake occurs, and the oversteepened, cracked north slope collapses. Three large slide blocks create the debris avalanche, exposing the cryptodome and releasing the confined pressure. Superheated water within the volcano flashes to steam and an enormous lateral blast occurs.

D. The blast cloud expands rapidly and is directed northward out of the horseshoe-shaped crater. The blast's energy is equivalent to 20 million tons of TNT. Total volume of the avalanche rubble is 3.3 billion cubic yards (2.5 billion cubic meters).

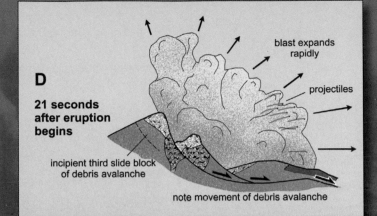

D

21 seconds after eruption begins

blast expands rapidly

projectiles

incipient third slide block of debris avalanche

note movement of debris avalanche

E. After one minute of eruption, the 930ºC magma begins to jet from 10-kilometers depth through the nozzle below the crater to form a spectacular "Plinian" eruption. This column collapses to form pyroclastic flows which stream northward at high velocity from the crater.

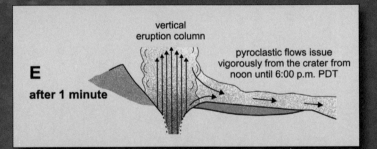

E

after 1 minute

vertical eruption column

pyroclastic flows issue vigorously from the crater from noon until 6:00 p.m. PDT

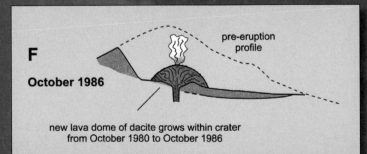

F

October 1986

pre-eruption profile

new lava dome of dacite grows within crater from October 1980 to October 1986

F. After six magmatic eruptions, the steam pressure is low enough for dacite magma to be intruded without large explosions into the swelling dome within the crater. Between October 18, 1980 and October 26, 1986, seventeen episodes of dome growth add 74 million cubic meters of dacite to this third and newest dome. Dome height by 1986 is 1,150 feet (350 meters) and the elevation of the crater's south rim is 8,363 feet (2,549 meters).

Animals frequently exhibit an uncanny ability to sense impending danger and migrate out of harm's way. In the days before the eruption, many of the large animals on the north side of the mountain migrated away from the path of the northward directed blast. They seemed to know when it was going to blow and which direction was in jeopardy, even though geophysicists could not fully discern the signs.

Within a few short minutes, the incredible beauty of the mountain had been stripped away. In its place remained an open wound in the earth's surface within an area of about 230 square miles (600 square kilometers). The initial explosion of the mountain released the energy equivalent of 20 million tons of TNT. The total energy output during the nine-hour eruption on May 18 was equivalent to 440 million tons of TNT, approximately 30,000 Hiroshima atomic bombs.

Sunday, May 18, 1980, began like many other late-spring days at the volcano. At 8:32 a.m. the sky was clear, sensors installed by scientists were in position all around the volcano, and people were impatiently waiting for the big explosion with cameras in hand. The explosion happened in broad daylight — not a cloud in the sky — while eyewitnesses observed from several positions.

Some observers, fifty-seven in all including some scientific observers, were too close and perished. Thankfully, the restricted-zone signs placed by the government persuaded most people to stay away, and loggers, fortunately, had Sunday off. Abundant observations by those outside the devastation zone allowed geologists to piece together a detailed chronology of events at the volcano.

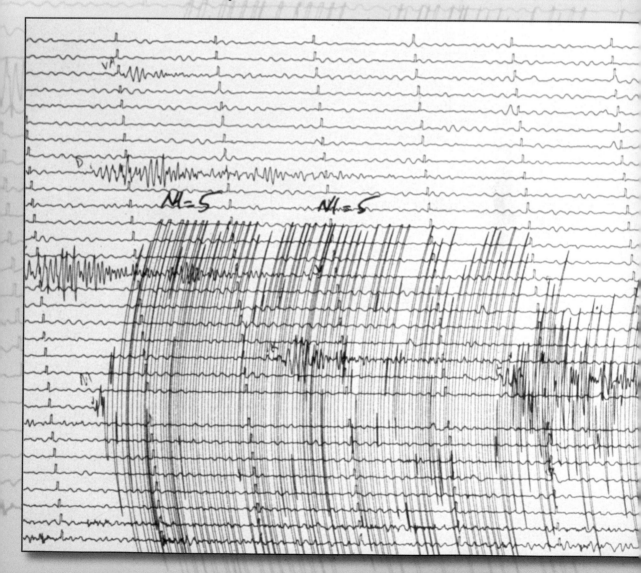

1) EARTHQUAKE

As two geologists flew their chartered plane over the summit of Mount St. Helens at 8:32 a.m., they saw rocks falling into the small summit crater. Little did they realize that deep inside the mountain magma movements and excessive pressures had triggered an earthquake which would shatter the tenuous tranquility.

The seismograph in Portland registered the time of the initial earthquake at seventeen seconds after 8:32 a.m. and calibrated it as 5.1 on the Richter scale. The two geologists observing the mountain from the airplane described the north slope as "rippling and churning" and wisely opted for a hasty departure.

2) DEBRIS AVALANCHE

Within seconds, the swollen and over-steepened north slope of the volcano transformed itself into the largest landslide recorded by man. The avalanche debris consisted of rock and ice that totaled about 3.3 billion cubic yards (2.5 billion cubic meters) and was launched northward off the summit in three distinct blocks (see Box C and D on pages 24-25). Lubricated by ice, water, and air, the debris reached speeds exceeding 150 miles per hour (240 kilometers per hour). Three-quarters of this avalanche rubble landed in the North Fork of the Toutle River, blocking the drainage basin. Much of it was deposited as hummocks and small hills on the landscape northwest of the volcano. The remaining one-fourth of the avalanche debris slammed into Spirit Lake north of the volcano.

Collapse of the summit and north slope of the volcano released the pent-up pressure within the mountain. Molten rock at 1700° F (930° C) literally exploded the water content into steam with energy equivalent to 20 million tons of TNT (about the size of the biggest nuclear bombs). Because the north slope of the volcano was now missing, the steam blast was directed northward over the landscape. The blast cloud moved as a hot ground-hugging atmospheric current at speeds over 650 miles per hour (300 meters per second) and destroyed 200 square miles (500 square kilometers) of forest within ten minutes. In some places, the blast attained supersonic speeds leaving distinct furrows on the ground surface. Photographs made at 10 miles (16 kilometers) distance from the mountain show large blocks of rock hurtling through the air within the blast cloud. Some projectiles landed miles from the crater.

When the volcano vented, blowing out to the north, the billowing cloud thrown into the air was not just rock particles; 90 percent of it was superheated water. Underground, the water had been maintained in liquid form due to the weight of the overburdened rock, but it flashed to steam as the pressures were released when the bulge fell away. This immediate change from superheated water to steam precipitated a huge volume increase causing an explosive eruption. No liquid lava flowed out in this volcanic eruption, as it does when less water is present in the magma, but the devastation was no less dramatic.

The steam explosion created three distinct zones. Near the volcano, trees, rocks, and soil were ripped loose and became part of the blast. Farther away trees were toppled by the intensity of the blast, their trunks pointing away from the volcano. At the distant margin of the blast zone, trees remained standing but were scorched, leaving a grim skeleton of a forest. The northward-directed steam explosion was one of the most unexpected aspects of the May 18 eruption. Geologists learned the important lesson — lateral as well as vertical blasts can occur at volcanoes.

As the steam explosion passed over the landscape north of the volcano, the next extraordinary stage of events occurred. The 680 million cubic yards (500 million cubic meters) of debris avalanche material that landed in Spirit Lake basin formed a gigantic water wave when it displaced the water of the lake northward. The lake was propelled as a wave or series of waves to a height of 860 feet (260 meters) on the hillsides north of the lake. No cameras recorded the water wave, but the water-scoured zone can be clearly seen on the eroded slopes north of Spirit Lake. As the water rushed back into its basin, an estimated one million large trees that had occupied the slopes north of the lake collected as an enormous floating log mat in Spirit Lake. The first National Guard helicopter pilots who observed the lake's surface late in the afternoon of May 18 could not distinguish water between the floating logs. It looked like the lake was missing. When everything settled down, the water became visible; but the floor of the lake was found to be 300 feet (90 meters) higher than it had been before the eruption because so much sediment had been introduced. Things had forever changed.

5) MUDFLOWS

Within the first few hours, snow and ice melted by the intense heat of the blast descended the mountain, sweeping up soil, rocks and trees to form mudflows within six major drainage basins surrounding the volcano. On the flank of the volcano, mudflows moved at 90 miles per hour (145 kilometers per hour), slowing down when arriving at the river channels. Many river valleys were completely filled with mud. Dozens of bridges were washed away. During the late afternoon of May 18, homes and businesses were overcome by the cement-like slurry in areas where people supposed they were at low risk. Mud even choked the channel of the mighty Columbia River, halting river traffic for days.

During (May 18, 1980- March 19, 1982)

Debris avalanche and steam explosion formed the horseshoe-shaped crater. Goat Rocks area was replaced by Step Canyon and Loowit Canyon. The North Fork of the Toutle River was blocked by a massive debris deposit creating a poorly integrated drainage basin. Steam explosion pits formed on the pumice plain north of the crater. Spirit Lake basin received an average thickness of 300 feet (90 meters) of avalanche debris. The lake had no natural outlet, and was over 250 feet (76 meters) higher and nearly twice the area as before the eruption. On Coldwater Creek and Castle Creek, new lakes formed behind smaller debris dams. To view earlier and later configurations, see maps on pages 21 and 53.

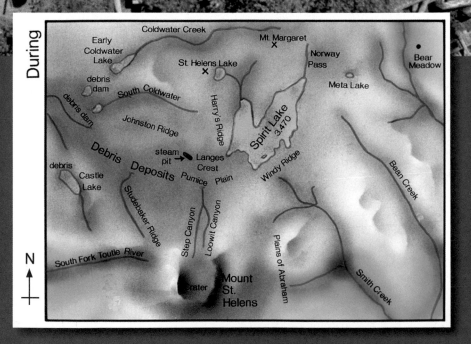

During

Coldwater Creek

Early Coldwater Lake

Mt. Margaret ×

Norway Pass

Bear Meadow

St. Helens Lake ×

debris dam

South Coldwater

Meta Lake

debris dam

Johnston Ridge

Harry's Ridge

Spirit Lake 3470

Debris Deposits

steam pit

Langes Crest

debris

Castle Lake

Pumice Plain

Windy Ridge

Bean Creek

Studebaker Ridge

Step Canyon

Loowit Canyon

Plains of Abraham

Smith Creek

N

South Fork Toutle River

Crater

Mount St. Helens

With the steam blast exhausted, the next phase of the eruption began. Magma from 6 miles (10 kilometers) beneath the volcano was being propelled upward through a nozzle within the crater. As entrained water expanded into steam, it frothed the magma into small rock particles called pumice (volcanic ash). A gigantic plume of pumice and volcanic gas inflated over the summit of the volcano late in the morning and early afternoon of May 18. The images of this "Plinian eruption" made the front pages of newspapers and magazines as this plume

intermittently filled and collapsed within the crater. Each time the plume collapsed, especially during the afternoon, the walls of the crater directed ground-hugging "rivers" of hot, fluidized volcanic ash northward over the landscape near the volcano. These "rivers" of hot volcanic ash, known to geologists as "pyroclastic flows," consist of particles slurried along by volcanic gas, not water, and move at freeway speeds. Today a "pumice plain" seen north of the volcano, bears testimony to the deposits of pyroclastic flows that blanketed the area during the afternoon of May 18.

7) Air Fall Tephra

Pumice fragments continued to fall throughout the nine-hour eruption on May 18. The collective term for all coarse and fine volcanic ash particles lofted through the atmosphere and accumulated at the earth's surface is "tephra." More than two-tenths cubic

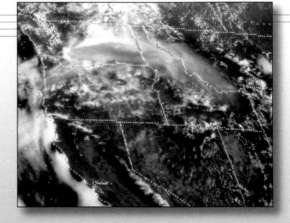

Afternoon, May 18

9:15 a.m., May 18

mile (one cubic kilometer) of tephra carpeted the region, and winds that day carried the finest ash eastward into Idaho, Montana, Wyoming, and beyond, affecting weather around the globe. The weather satellite recorded images of the northwest from 22,000 miles (35,000 kilometers) above the volcano.

Total Devastation

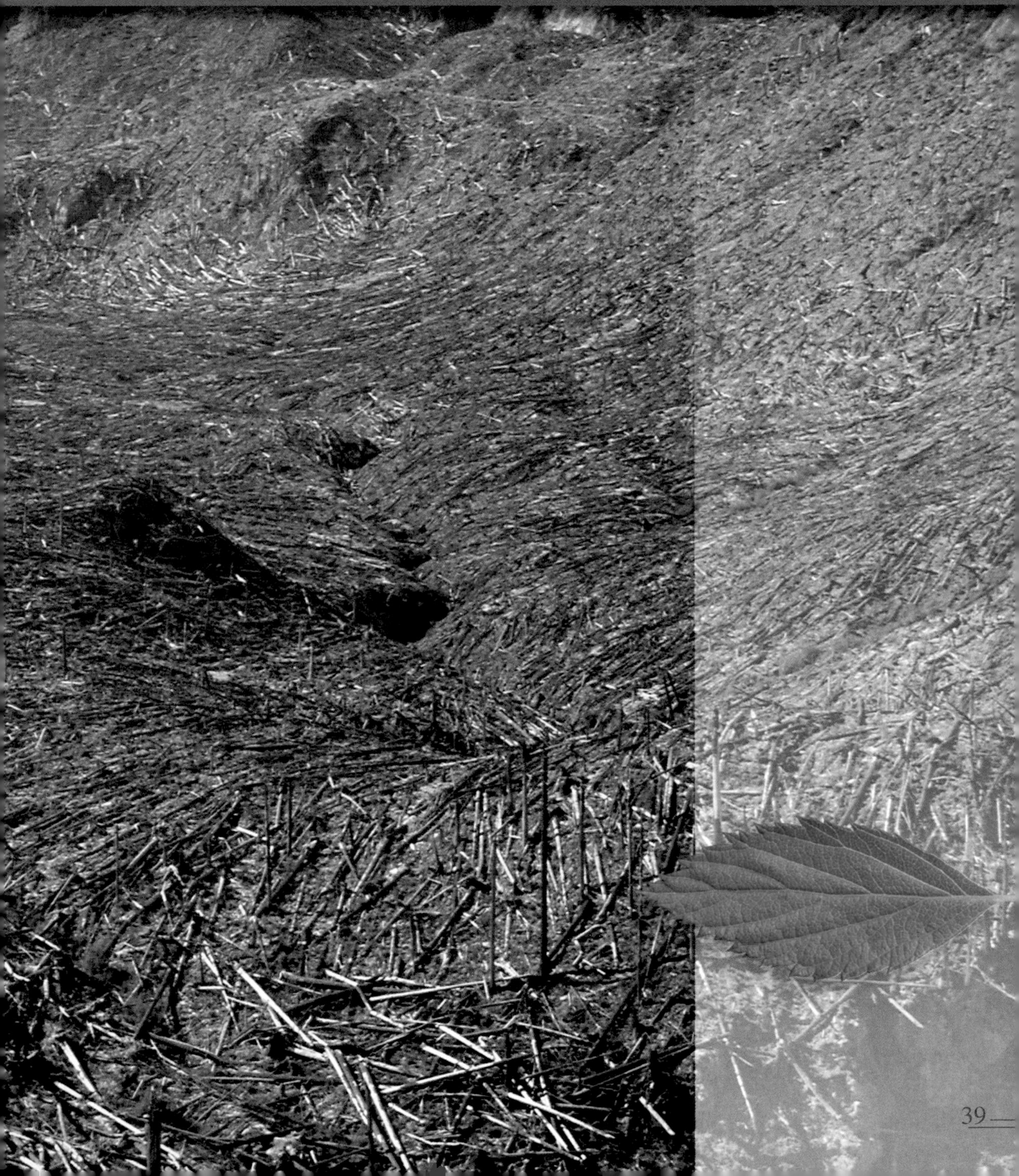

The blast cloud, billowing away from the mountain and traveling at an initial speed of over 650 miles per hour (300 meters per second) forcefully uprooted or snapped off trees within the blast zone. As it swirled through the hills, trees were wrenched from the ground and dropped pointing away from the mountain. Nearly 3 billion board-feet of timber were leveled within ten minutes. That much timber could be used to build 640,000 houses. Areas on the fringes were scorched. In the wake of the blast cloud, 230 square miles (600 square kilometers) of previously forested area had been transformed into a barren windblown desert.

Because blast temperatures exceeded 500° F (260° C), all twigs, leaves, and similar structures along with the small animal population simply ceased to exist. Only the thick trunks and larger branches remained. In recent years, a road has been built which provides access to the outer blast zone, now contained within a national monument.

The surrealist "fingerprint" pattern, covering as far as the eye can see with tree trunks oriented in the same direction, speaks eloquently of the power involved in the eruption.

STEAM EXPLOSION PITS

The debris avalanche, the venting steam, the flowing mud, and the pyroclastic flows, all moved at high velocities. Each left a deposit of sediments behind as it passed or halted. Today we see these pancake-like deposits in a stack measuring up to 600 feet (180 meters) thick.

Ice within the landslide deposit was covered by very hot volcanic ash north of the volcano.

Buried ice or water quickly turned to steam, usually slowly venting through cracks. When the pressure built up too quickly, it exploded to the surface. Today we see numerous "steam explosion pits," some of renowned sizes. Those holes, reamed through the still soft, recently deposited pancake-like layers, look much like craters on the moon.

May 23, 1980

SCOUR SLOPE

That extremely energetic wave, caused by the avalanche of 680 million cubic yards (500 million cubic meters) of rock and mud into Spirit Lake, raced northerly across the lake and slammed into the mountain slope on the opposite side. As the waters sloshed up and then came back down, they completely scoured the slope to a height of 860 feet (260 meters) above the original lake level. The returning waters scoured off the trees, leaves, animals, and soil and even eroded deep ruts into the hard bedrock of the hillside. Geologists call such an eroded slope a "scour slope" and marvel that it was stripped so thoroughly in such a short amount of time. This scour slope was formed in less than one minute!

So much sediment entered the lake that the bottom of the lake is now higher than the surface of the lake had been before. Needless to say, all fish in the lake itself were casualties either of the impact, the shock wave, or the choking, searing sediments. Nothing survived.

The eruption spewed volcanic ash 12 miles (19 kilometers) high into the air, where it was dispersed by the winds. Eventually, it fell like snow, and formed a slippery clay-like layer that caused much damage. In places, it completely blocked out the sun at mid-day, causing the streetlights to turn on at noon. Residents near the mountain found themselves in almost total blackness. Many feared for their lives.

The grit in the air to the east of the mountain greatly affected machinery and cars. As air filters became clogged, the destructive grit entered the engines. Disabled and wrecked cars sat everywhere. For weeks, snowplows pushed volcanic ash off the roads like snow.

50X

100X

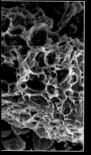

1000X

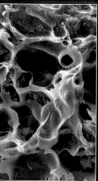

Ash magnified by a scanning electron micrograph.

Mudflows, following quickly on the heels of the avalanche and pyroclastic flows, scooped up everything in their path. They consisted of melted snow and ice from the now hot summit, along with soil, rocks, and trees. These extremely dense mudflows, with the consistency of cement flowing from a cement truck, caused more devastation than we can imagine. Flowing at such high speeds, nothing could stand in their path — not even large trees, buildings, or bridges. Logging camps were destroyed, equipment was strewn around, and the logs were tossed like toothpicks.

Several such flows occurred during the initial day of the eruption; others followed over the next several years, as lesser eruptions melted any new snow that had subsequently accumulated near the crater. The mudflow of March 19, 1982, is pictured to the right.

The flows continued for many miles down through the drainage basin to lower elevations. Witnesses said that the flowing mud resembled rapids in a river. It filled the valleys and left a "bathtub ring" behind.

Height of mud

GEOLOGIC DEPOSITS

HOW PARTICLES SEPARATE TO FORM STRATA

Before the eruption of Mount St. Helens, geologists considered models of strata formation within uniformitarian constraints. Thin stratification (technically called lamination) was thought to form very slowly, as sediment was delivered by rather sluggish agents. The boundaries between consecutive strata were often deemed to represent long-time breaks with no deposition.

At Mount St. Helens, we saw a living laboratory for the rapid formation of strata. An abundance of coarse and fine particles was produced by the explosive eruptions. Pyroclastic flows, mudflows, and river floods distributed the particles widely and accumulated strata in a hurry. We learned that the flow process creates a sweeping action as particles roll or bounce along at Earth's surface, quickly separating the particles by size, shape and density and forming even micro-thin laminae. Particles with similar size, shape, or density are deposited together at a specific horizon within the bed. Each moving particle requires a specific energy level to transport it. When that energy level is exceeded, the flow is able to winnow and segregate the larger particles from the finer ones within the moving flow. Below that energy level, deposition occurs.

The sequence of events at Mount St. Helens produced three significant types of stratification: (1) horizontal lamination, (2) cross-bedding, and (3) graded massive beds.

Horizontal Lamination

Thin layers of sediment with very fine particles occur as layers usually much less than one-quarter-inch (0.5 centimeter) thick. This thin stratification was produced by particles rolling and bouncing at high speed within gas- or water-charged, low-density flows, especially pyroclastic flows.

Cross-bedding

Thicker layers of coarser sediment with internal, inclined lamination occur in association with both dilute mudflows and lower density pyroclastic flows. This type of stratification was formed by moderate-speed flows that sculpted dunes on the depositional surface.

Graded Massive Beds

Some thicker layers of coarser sediment appear to possess internally a rather homogeneous texture. With closer study, however, these beds display a progressive particle size variation upward within the bed, with larger particles on the bottom grading into finer particles above. This type of stratification was produced by fast-moving, high-density mudflows and pyroclastic flows. Some of these flows were laminar whereas others were turbulent. Most particles were carried by suspension within a slurried medium, without significant rolling or bouncing of particles. These beds accumulated very rapidly as decreasing energy and internal friction suddenly halted movement.

RAPID SEDIMENTATION

Three distinct layers can be seen in this cliff face, which consists of the upper 60 feet (20 meters) of a 600-foot (180 meters) deposit. The cliff face is the exposed side of a breached steam explosion pit. The lowest zone is made up of ash fall material altered and sorted by the steam explosion which exposed this cliff. The central layer dates from the June 12, 1980,

90-miles-per-hour (150-kilometers-per-hour) pyroclastic flow consisting of hot gas and pumice fragments. Note its distinctive bedded nature. The upper layer was formed by a 40-miles-per-hour (60-kilometers-per-hour) mudflow on March 19, 1982.

Keep in mind that this is just the upper portion of a much thicker deposit. Geologists normally think that it takes excessively long periods of time to accumulate such thick sequences of sediments. In this picture, however, we see three episodes of rapid sedimentation recorded; each one took minutes to hours instead of long periods of time to form.

Mudflow deposit, March 19, 1982

Pyroclastic flow deposit, late evening June 12, 1980

Air fall tephra, Afternoon May 18, 1980

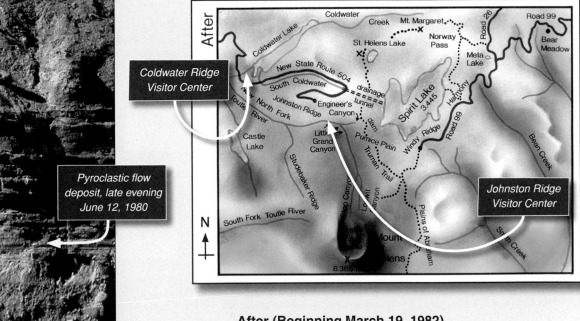

Coldwater Ridge Visitor Center

Johnston Ridge Visitor Center

After (Beginning March 19, 1982)

Mudflows had caused an integrated drainage pattern with canyons to be established through the debris which had blocked the valley of the North Fork of the Toutle River. Coldwater and Castle Lakes were stabilized. The level of Spirit Lake was lowered by the drainage tunnel drilled through Harry's Ridge. Roads and trails were constructed. A large lava dome became stabilized inside the crater. To view earlier configurations, see maps on pages 21 and 35.

The bedding within the central layer, deposited within three hours by the 90-miles-per-hour (150-kilometers-per-hour) pyroclastic flow, clearly resembles the character of many rock units in other areas. Geologists normally interpret such beds as having been deposited over long periods of time, usually in rather calm environments.

Close-up of pyroclastic flow deposit from Mount St. Helens eruption

The Redwall Limestone stands as a recognizable vertical cliff in the Grand Canyon, about midway between the river and the rim. Water flowing from the reddish Supai siltstone and then over the Redwall stains the cliff red and gives it its name. Uniformitarians have long considered limestone to have formed slowly, as particles of calcium carbonate accumulated under a calm, placid sea. Recently, however, gradation of particles as well as a cross-bedding has been discovered within the layers. The Redwall appears to be better interpreted as the result of a series of rapid, high density, underwater sediment flows covering much of the American southwest.

Redwall Limestone in the Grand Canyon

The Tapeats Sandstone in the Grand Canyon, similar in many respects to deposits at Mount St. Helens, has traditionally been interpreted as taking long ages to accumulate on the floor of a calm ocean. By better understanding catastrophic processes, leading geologists have also recently reinterpreted it. The Tapeats is now understood to be the result of a series of dynamic underwater currents. Conventional geologists believe that it formed some 550 million years ago. Flood geologists, on the other hand, suspect that the Tapeats was one of the early deposits of Noah's flood.

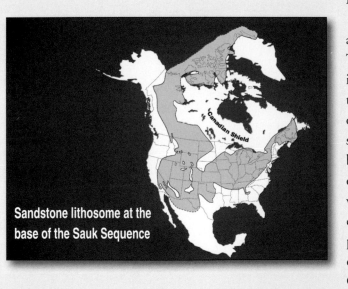

Sandstone lithosome at the base of the Sauk Sequence

When the areal extent of the Tapeats Sandstone is plotted, we see that this series of underwater sediment flows blanketed much of the continent when the ocean covered a large portion of the continent. Catastrophic deposits covering a large region are common in the geologic record. Biblical catastrophism would predict exactly that!

The pumice fragments deposited by the eruption looked and behaved much like ordinary sand grains. Here is a question: how long does it take for soft, sandy sediments to harden into sedimentary rock? Students are taught that it takes excessively long periods of time.

Studies show that solidification speeds up when high confining pressure forces the grains together and squeezes out excess water. Elevated temperature helps too. However, the primary factor in hardening sediments is the presence of a cementing agent, which binds the grains and molecules together, much like cement binds sand and gravel together into a hard concrete.

At Mount St. Helens the conditions were far from ideal, but the near vertical slope in this photograph taken in 1985 consists of sediments deposited in 1980 and 1982. The canyon itself was eroded when, in an effort to stabilize Spirit Lake, the lake level was lowered by pumping. The outflow easily cut through the recently deposited sediments. Exposed to air, no longer saturated, and not under very great pressure — hardly ideal conditions, but in less than five years, the sediments were solidified enough that they could stand at a near vertical slope, something only rather hard rock can do. It does not take long ages to form rock. It just takes the right conditions.

A clastic rock is formed when small pieces of a previous deposit are eroded and redeposited. For example, sand grains make up sandstone, which is classified as a clastic rock. A dike of such material is formed when grains or soft sediments are displaced from an unconsolidated source, fill in a fissure, and take on the fissure's tabular shape.

These dikes on Mount St. Helens were emplaced, grain by grain, as steam escaped from the hot muds, and

Dikes near Rockwall, Texas

These sandstone dikes intrude into a limestone bed in central Texas. The date normally assigned to the source sandstone bed below is millions of years older than the date at which the sandy material was squeezed up like toothpaste. The source rock must still have been soft to allow such deformation. However, the time required for a sandy deposit to turn into hard, solid sandstone — in ideal conditions like this with the nearby presence of abundant calcite cement in the limestone — is not long; at most, it is only a few hundred years. Something seems to be wrong with the timing.

rushed upward through cracks in the overlying sediments. Steam-propelled sand coated the inside of the fissure, growing thicker as the process continued. Once pressures were relieved, a vertical dike, or wall-like feature, remained, easily identified by its different texture.

Later, after they had hardened, they were exposed by erosion as the canyon deepened and widened.

The granite body which is buckled up to form Pike's Peak also serves, in many locations, as the core of the Rocky Mountains. The sandstone dike pictured here originated when sandy sediments were injected into the older granite, flowing like caulk squirted into a crack. Here is the problem. The age normally assigned to the source sandstone bed is about 550 million years old. The time of injection, concurrent with the tilting and uplift associated with the formation of the Rocky Mountains, was about 70 million years ago — or so it is claimed. This means that the source bed was already about 480 million years old at the time of emplacement.

However, sandy sediments do not take excessively long

time periods to harden into sandstone, and the sandy material must still have been soft when injected; otherwise, they would show evidence of fracturing and recementing. Because they appear to have hardened for the first time where we now find them, they must have been rather recently deposited. The 480-million-year delay in the injection process is a myth.

Clastic dike in Rocky Mountains: Sawatch sandstone in Pike's Peak granite

LEFTOVERS FROM THE LOG JAM

Most of the monetary damage done at Mount St. Helens was actually due to log-choked mudflows, rushing downstream, overflowing river beds, and bashing into bridges and farmhouses in their path. Even miles from their source, the cement-like slurries raced along at speeds up to 40-miles-per-hour (60-kilometers-per-hour). Nothing could stand in their path. Many of the floating logs jostled along in an upright position. Their roots, which often contained rocks plucked up with the tree by the blast cloud, tended to sink below the flowing mud surface, while the tree trunk stuck up into the air. When the flowing mud finally came to a halt, many of the trees were still in an upright growth position far from their original growth location.

WATER-SORTED BEDS

Moving fluids tend to sort their sediment load out into layers. Particles which are denser and rounder settle out first, with lighter ones settling only as the velocity of the fluid decreases. It is normally thought that such bedding results from processes taking place in calm environments, such as when rivers enter a calm lake or flow into a river delta. Here at Mount St. Helens, rapid deposition produced well sorted beds. It did not take a long time.

Rapid Formation of Laminated Deposit

In some calm lake beds and offshore areas today, minute laminae called varves form each year as small particles accumulate. Each varve consists of a winter/summer couplet with recognizable chemistry and size differences for each season. If one assumes that slow and gradual processes have occurred exclusively throughout the past, counting the "yearly" deposits yields an estimate of the time it took to deposit the entire sequence. In some areas, millions of these varves are found in sequence, leading most geologists to postulate it took millions of years for them to form.

Scientists know that this assumption is not always reliable. Laboratory experiments have duplicated varves forming rapidly in depositional tanks. Furthermore, there are many natural examples where more than one varve has formed in one year. Despite this knowledge, the concept is still used as a teaching tool; and geologists often interpret varved deposits in this way, with each varve interpreted as a yearly deposit. At Mount St. Helens, varve-like laminae were formed by the multiplied thousands in a span of a few hours by fast-moving, gas-entrained, pyroclastic flows. Thin stratification also formed in the river flood flows.

Quicksand

The material comprising the sandy mudflows at Mount St. Helens was made not of the normal quartz sand grains but of the sand-grain-sized particles of pumice. It looks and behaves like a normal sand deposit. When saturated, it acts just like normal quicksand would act. Quicksand containing scalding-hot water could be encountered in canyons eroded through steam explosion pits five years after the main eruption. A "blanket" of overlying material maintained the heat for a time, but the hot sediments could not retain their heat indefinitely. After ten years, the water had lost much of its heat.

It is truly remarkable that in many places around the world, "hot-springs" are found where the underground, blanketed source of heat is thought to be many millions of years old. In some areas, the heat is continually restored from even deeper sources. In others there is no such source, and the buried layer is cooling. How could they have retained their heat for such long periods, only to lose the heat during the years

scientists have been keeping records? Hot springs resorts, whose waters are no longer sufficiently warm, are frequently abandoned. Are the assigned dates credible?

Often, as in the above picture, a crust forms on top of the deposit. When an unsuspecting researcher breaks through that crust the entire area suddenly transforms into scalding-hot quicksand. It is no wonder that the area is off-limits to tourists and restricted to scientists with research permits. Within a few more years, the danger will be over.

THE NEW LAVA DOME

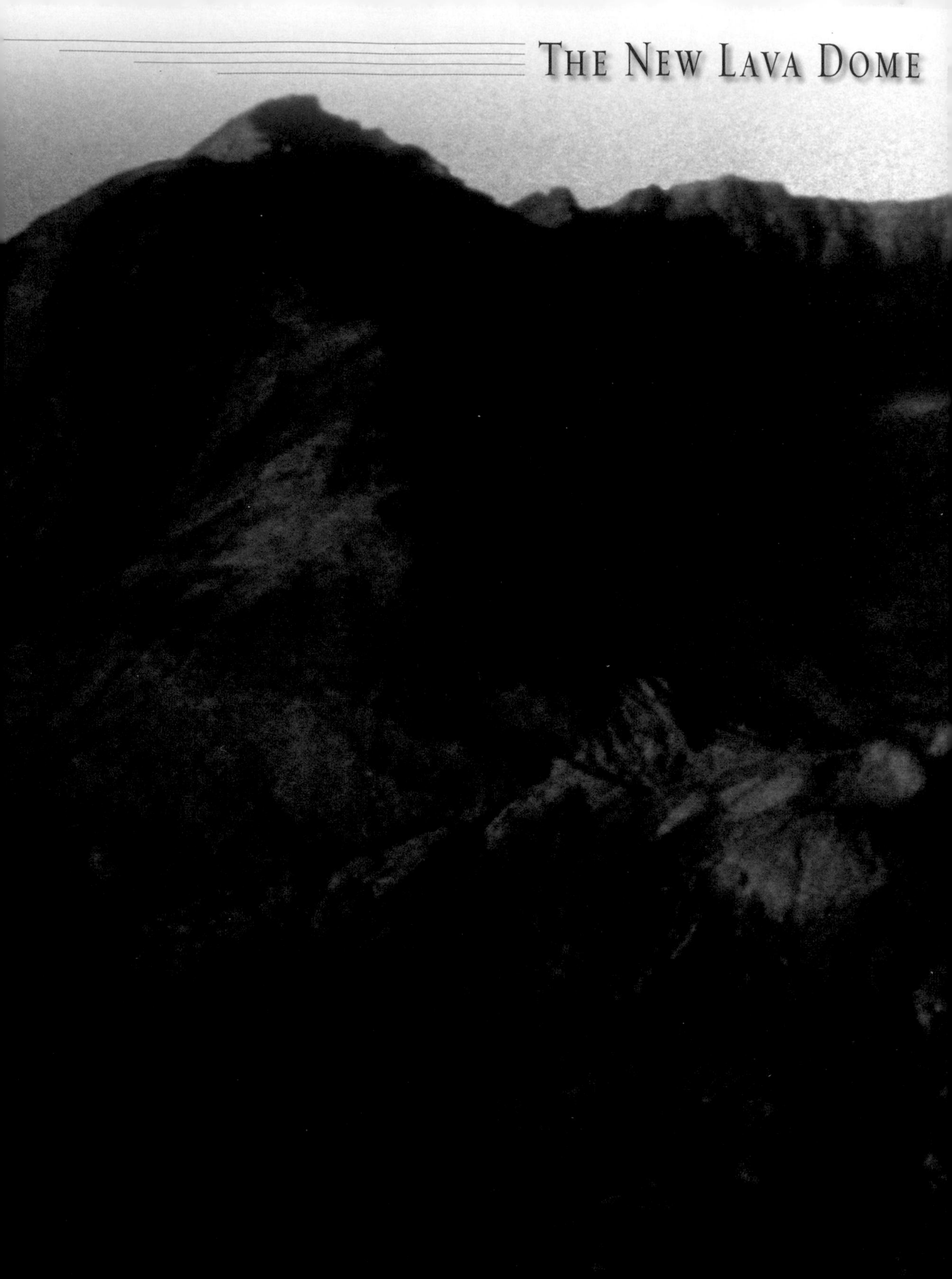

When the mountain erupted, it left a crater exposing the nozzle through which pulverized rock, water, and gas had been forced to the surface from the interior of the earth. However, within days following the five major eruptions, the pressures had been relieved and a dome of hardened lava began to build. Five times over the years, subsequent eruptions removed each growing lava dome. The present dome began to grow in October 1980 until growth halted in 1986. Measuring 876 feet (267 meters) high, it is still hot and unstable.

DATING THE LAVA DOME

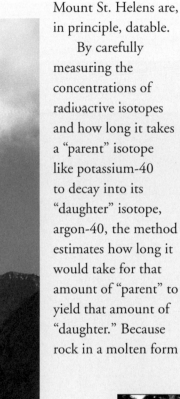

Radioisotope dating techniques claim to be able to determine the age of a rock. Only those rocks that were once in a hot molten condition, such as volcanic rocks, are candidates for radioisotope dating. Thus, the rocks at Mount St. Helens are, in principle, datable.

By carefully measuring the concentrations of radioactive isotopes and how long it takes a "parent" isotope like potassium-40 to decay into its "daughter" isotope, argon-40, the method estimates how long it would take for that amount of "parent" to yield that amount of "daughter." Because rock in a molten form would easily release gases like argon, the time calculated is really the time which has elapsed since the igneous material cooled from a hot, molten magma into a solid rock. This elapsed time is interpreted as the age of the rock.

Because potassium decays into argon very slowly, the rocks formed in and subsequent to the 1980 eruption at Mount St. Helens should date "too young to measure." Almost no "daughter" argon should be present.

Samples gathered have now been dated using the potassium-argon method. According to radioisotope dating, certain minerals in the lava dome are up to 2.4 million years old. All of the minerals combined yield the date of 350,000 years by the potassium-argon technique. However, we know that these minerals and the rocks that contain them cooled within lava between the years 1980 and 1986. This situation is not unique. Nearly every time a rock of known age has been dated by radioisotope dating, the calculated age is similarly exaggerated. Should we trust these methods to date rocks of unknown age?

Microscopic view of the crystals composing the lava dome

LANDFORMS

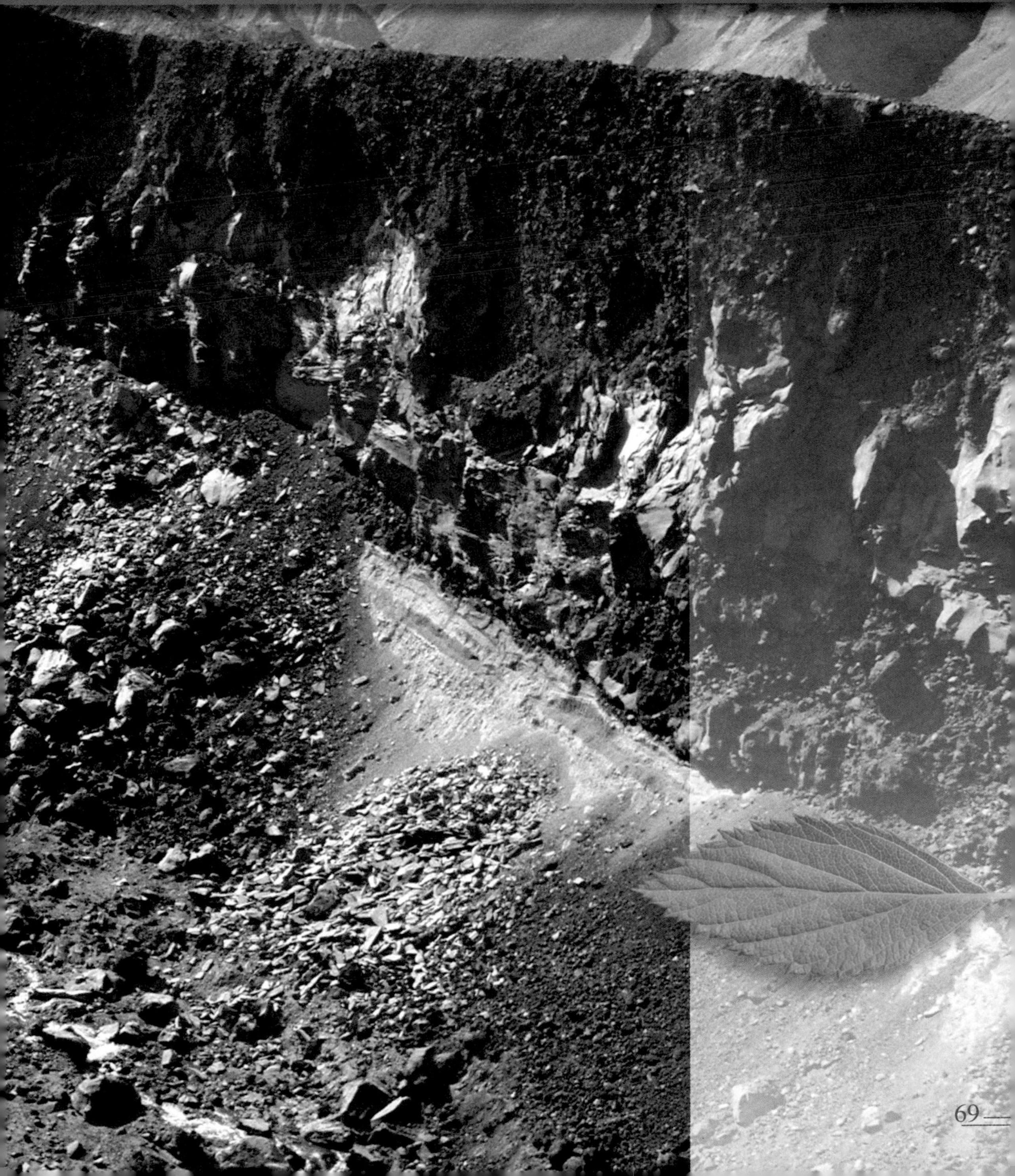

Rapid Erosion of a Canyon Through Solid Rock

How long would it take to erode a 100-foot (30-meter) deep canyon, in hard basaltic rock? On Mount St. Helens, such a canyon was formed rapidly as rock avalanched from the crater followed by other episodic, catastrophic processes.

Not much geologic work is done on a day-to-day basis by normal processes, but when enough energy is available to a system such that an "energy threshold" is crossed, extensive amounts of geologic work can be accomplished quickly. At Mount St. Helens, the "energy threshold" was crossed many times and in many ways.

Hard-rock erosion probably occurred by two energetic processes: (1) plucking and (2) cavitation. Plucking is the prying-apart action that loosens rock during large mudflows and water flows. Cavitation is a bubble-bursting process in very high-velocity flows that inflicts hammer-like blows which pulverize rocks.

RAPID GROOVING OF SOLID ROCK

Scratches in hard rock are often found in glaciated areas. They no doubt were scraped as the glacier slowly crept along.

At Mount St. Helens, identical grooves, or striations, resulted when the avalanche and blast cloud tore boulders from their places and hurled them down the mountain, dragging them with great force across exposed rock.

RAPID FORMATION OF BADLANDS TOPOGRAPHY

Once a steam explosion had occurred on the pumice plain and a steam explosion pit had formed, the edges of it were unstable and began to slough away until a stable slope was reached. Looking down from above, one

This topography reminds us of the Badlands of South Dakota and some of the deserts of the Southwestern United States. Geologists often suppose that badlands features take many thousands of years to develop.

June 18, 1980

can easily see an elaborate pattern of rills and gullies, looking very much like patterns of streams and rivers on a map. This erosion pattern is virtually identical to "badlands" topography found in dry, unvegetated areas.

In fact, these rills and gullies were formed in less than five days, after the steam explosion pit was reamed out. Usually water is the erosive agent. Here it was gravity, shaping unconsolidated sediments into a stable slope.

Rapid Formation of River Canyons

Twenty-three square miles (60 square kilometers) of the old valley of the North Fork of the Toutle River were choked by landslide and debris avalanche material on May 18. The upper river was completely buried by up to 600 feet (180 meters) of avalanche debris which blocked the old valley. For almost two years, the upper drainage basin around Spirit Lake was isolated from its previous drainage into the Toutle River. Geologists and engineers were very concerned about the stability of the debris dam in the Langes Crest area. How

would this material erode and how would the new drainage of the North Fork of the Toutle River be established across this large area? The answer to this question was not just of academic concern; the lives of people and the security of property downstream was at stake.

Geologists had been accustomed to thinking that river drainages were established across upland areas slowly by branching and dividing of gullies. According to theory, gullies should enlarge, deepen, and erode headward into the upland surface. As a result of such a slow evolutionary process, a dendritic drainage basin with a river would be re-established. Such a process, it was supposed, could take a million years.

Engineers, however, were thinking differently. They were concerned by the short-term threat posed by the debris dam. Could instability of the material cause the debris dam to be breached? The engineers were especially concerned about catastrophic drainage of Spirit Lake. The water level of Spirit Lake had been rising for two years, and the dam at the lake's southwest corner could rupture.

What happened next surprised all who were watching. On March 19, 1982, a small summit eruption melted snow within the crater and displaced water forming a 20-mile-long (32-kilometer) mudflow. The mudflow pooled within the big steam explosion pit behind the debris dam. Mud quickly overtopped the west end of the big steam pit and cut back and downward, producing a 140-foot-deep (43-meter) canyon where before there was no canyon. In a single day the new drainage channel of the North Fork of the Toutle River was established westward through the debris dam by a catastrophic mudflow!

The canyon produced by the mud has been called "The Little Grand Canyon" because it appears to be a one-fortieth scale model of the Grand Canyon of Arizona. The new canyon, like its famous precursor, has flat areas in highland surfaces on both sides, gully-headed side canyons, and enlarged cup-shaped side canyons. Fortunately the mudflow of March 19

did not erode the southwest corner of Spirit Lake; for then the rapid outflow of water would have devastated the basin below.

Geologists and engineers, who witnessed the March 19, 1982 mudflow and its rapid canyon-forming process, were greatly concerned about the stability of Spirit Lake. The Army Corps of Engineers declared a "state of emergency," installed a temporary pipeline over the debris dam, and began pumping the water of the lake over the debris dam. During the 28 months of pumping, the outflow from the pipe created another side canyon through the debris dam. This new canyon was called "Engineer's Canyon." The pipe was retired after Spirit Lake was lowered 25 feet (8 meters) when a drainage tunnel began operation in September 1985.

How would a geologic investigator understand the debris dam on the North Fork of the Toutle River if he knew nothing of its recent history? A geologic investigator would likely suppose that the steam explosion pit and the "Little Grand Canyon" positioned through it formed a long time ago and has continued to be shaped by an extended process of very gradual erosion. Such a conclusion would be in error. The landscape north of the volcano has been shaped by catastrophic agents that operated over very short periods of time.

GRAND CANYON

The Grand Canyon surely deserves its status as one of the great wonders of the natural world. We see it today, 250 miles long, 18 miles wide and 1 mile deep (400 kilometers long, 30 kilometers wide, and 2 kilometers deep) and wonder how it formed. No one saw it form; we just observe the way it exists in the present.

Most people are taught that the Colorado River eroded the Grand Canyon, down cutting for 70 million years as the Kaibab Plateau continued to rise. Even though this idea continues to dominate our textbooks, it has been abandoned by most geologists who actively research the canyon. An alternative viewpoint today is that the canyon was formed fairly recently in a much more rapid fashion by a dramatic water catastrophe. Some geologists suspect that the Grand Canyon was eroded by catastrophic drainage of lakes to the northeast. The upwarped plateau in northern Arizona does appear to have been a gigantic dam and the remnant of a muddy lake bottom can be seen. Does rapid erosion at Mount St. Helens provide a model to help explain the Grand Canyon?

Deposits in Spirit Lake

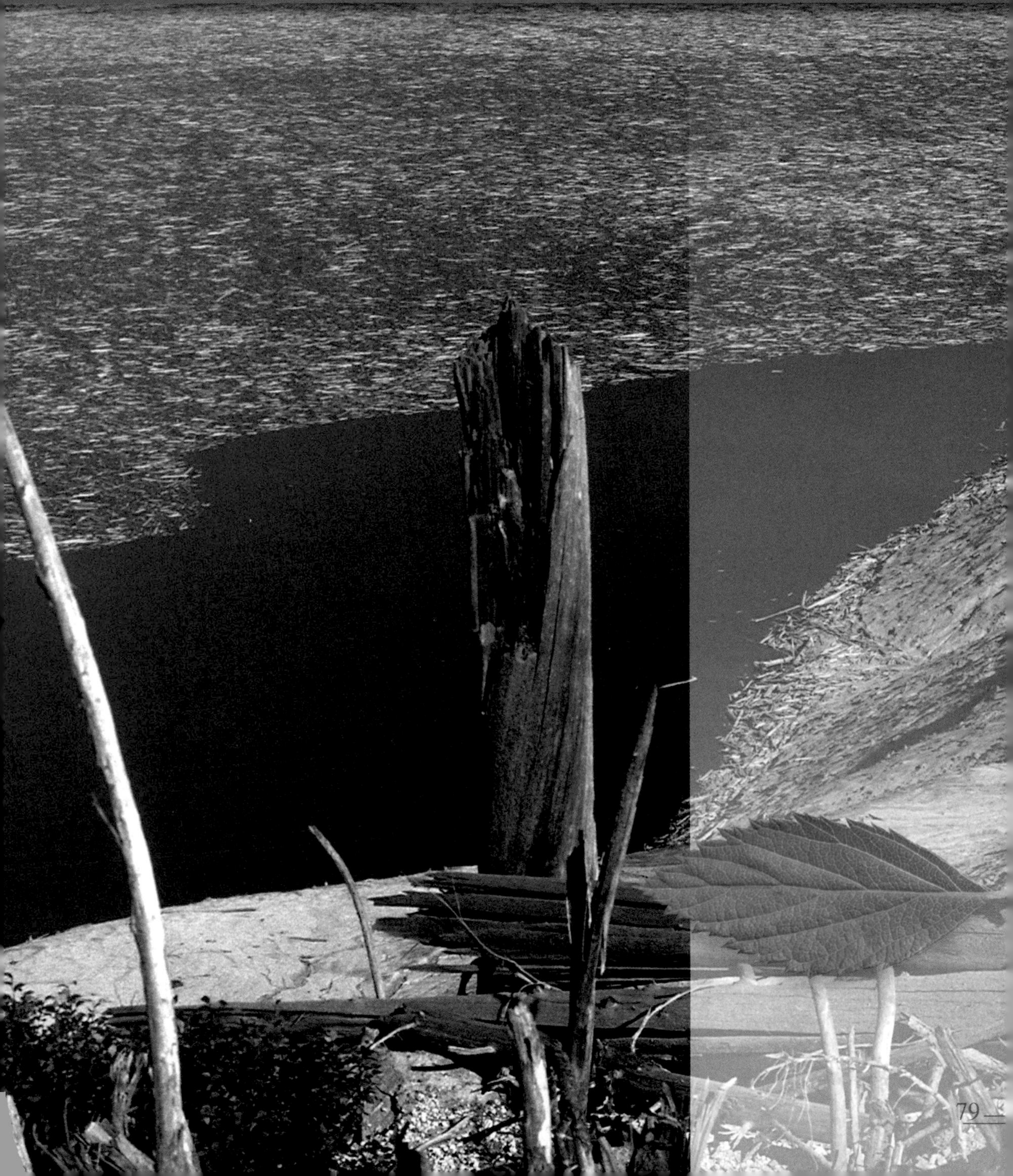

Structural Changes in the Lake

The huge earthquake-triggered avalanche that initiated the 1980 eruption descended the mountain's north side, depositing great thicknesses of sediments at the base of the mountain. Much of the avalanche found its way into Spirit Lake. When it was over, the floor of Spirit Lake was at a higher elevation than the surface of the lake had been before. The new lake was held in place by a tenuous dam made up of hummocky avalanche debris. Scientists were quite concerned that the mud dam would break, sending a second catastrophe downstream and overwhelming the towns below. As soon as possible, the Army Corps of Engineers began drilling a tunnel through bedrock to lower the lake to a more stable level. Pumping lowered it some 25 feet (8 meters). This was completed in 1985, leaving a raised shoreline behind.

Along many lakes worldwide as well as along the ocean, one can still see the remnants of previously raised shorelines. At Mount St. Helens the old shoreline was not only visible but a number of logs that had been floating were stranded at the higher level and now sit above the water.

VERTICAL CLIFF AT LAKE'S EDGE

I n many places a vertical cliff rimmed Spirit Lake. Such cliffs are often seen along shorelines where ocean waves have battered the shore and chemicals have etched the rock. It is thought that it takes a long time for such a sea cliff to form.

The Spirit Lake cliff was formed in hard basaltic rock in less than three years. This impressive erosion was exposed as the lake's immediate post-eruption water level was dropped and stabilized 25 feet (8 meters) lower than it had been before. Lesson: it does not take a long time to form a shoreline cliff; it just takes the right conditions.

On May 19, 1980, as soon as visibility increased and investigators could actually see the results of the eruption, they were concerned that Spirit Lake had disappeared. Only gradually did they realize that Spirit Lake still existed but that a floating mat of over one million logs covered it and obscured their view. The logs entered the lake not only with the avalanche but also when the resulting enormous wave dislodged and washed in the surrounding forest. Today, as the wind shifts, the logs float together across the lake as a thick log mat.

Creationists suggest that during Noah's flood, log mats like this may have yielded a deposit of broken plant debris called peat, the precursor to coal.

Swamp, southeastern United States

Geologists have long conjectured that coal seams are the altered remains of organic deposits known as peat, which collected under the stagnant waters of a swamp. Usually swamps are situated fairly close to sea level. The model supposes that from time to time the ocean level would rise and cover low-lying parts of the continents, including the swamps. Once under water, ocean sediments would collect above the submerged peat, eventually burying the peat deposit under a thick overburden.

In some areas, more than fifty layers of coal lie interspersed with marine sediments. Thus, geologists conclude that such an area may have been a swamp, above the water at one time and submerged beneath the oceans at a later time. Then, after great ages had seen the accumulation of thick layers of oceanic sediments covering the peat, the area rose above the oceans to become a swamp again. This cycle repeated scores of times. It is proposed that millions of years of heat and pressure due to deep burial might gradually metamorphose peat into coal.

We now know that coal does not necessarily take a long time to form. In recent years, numerous laboratory experiments have been devised in which coal is formed in a matter of minutes, hours, or days. Heat is the primary requirement to accomplish this transformation. The process is accelerated with the presence of volcanic clay known as montmorillinite or kaolinite, either which catalyzes the process. Moderate pressure enhances the process rate.

We generally think of swamps as rather flat-lying, but every swamp includes areas of elevated land interspersed by shallow water channels. Often found at the terminus of a river, swamps are laced with "distributaries" and levees. No laterally continuous flat surface can be found. Trees, bushes and small plants grow in abundance and the peat is laced with roots.

Yet today, coals almost always exhibit an exceedingly flat nature, and sharp contacts between it and marine strata above and below. Surely, modern coals did not derive from swamps similar to those of today.

Modern coals are also notoriously contaminated with volcanic ash or clay. Clay present with the original peat catalyzed its rapid transformation into coal.

When coal is burned in a furnace one must come back later and remove the "clinkers." Those clinkers are the clay and mineral matter that did not burn.

Two flat-lying coal seams of regular thickness interspersed with marine sediment — very different from modern peat deposits.

How did the great seams of coal form? Creationists have speculated that coal may have been formed as a result of Noah's flood, during which massive amounts of vegetation were scraped from the continents. Floating as a mat of vegetation on the world ocean, logs would have abraded against each other and decayed, accumulating a peat deposit beneath the floating mat. During the Flood year, abundant volcanic action produced clays which mixed in with peat. Subsequent deep burial by oceanic muds would have applied the pressure and heat needed to alter them rapidly into coal. A cycle of such decay, deposition, and metamorphism produced the multiple layers of coal that we see in the geologic record.

Unfortunately, no such floating mat existed for creationists to study — until Mount St. Helens erupted, that is. We have been studying it ever since.

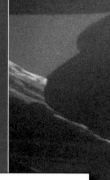

FLOATING MAT MODEL FOR ORIGIN OF COAL

FLOATING MAT

TRANSGRESSING SEA

CLAY

PEAT

ORGANIC-RICH MUD

*Underwater photos
of floating log mat*

Rapid Formation of Peat

Even though the waters of Spirit Lake were inhospitable to life, scuba divers ventured to the bottom of the lake underneath the floating log mat and discovered a deposit of peat at least three feet thick. The deposit consists of sheets of bark abraded from the floating logs above and decaying remnants of leaves, branches and water-soaked trunks mixed together in a matrix of soil and volcanic ash. Everything is present for a good peat.

Another eruption of Mount St. Helens might some day bury this peat under a hot layer of lava or volcanic ash. If it did, all of the requirements for rapid coalification would be present.

TYPICAL COAL

Coal typically consists of a variety of constituent parts. Looking at it carefully in cross section, you can distinctly see several types of layers. Some are shiny and hard, composed of "vitrain" bands, the decayed remnants of bark sheets. Others are the decayed remains of woody fibers, still others of leaves and various tissue. Some are thought to have been charred by fire. Usually present are thin, laterally extensive "clay partings," which are made up of volcanic ash. Often an unusual clay layer called an "underclay" lies beneath the coal.

Peat swamps exist today, but where is peat observed changing into coal? We wonder if the standard model is correct. Swamp peats of today do not look like they could turn into a common type of coal, but the peat at Spirit Lake seems to be an adequate precursor of a normal coal bed. Today's peats have a texture resembling "mashed potatoes," thoroughly penetrated by roots, whereas modern coals exhibit coarser textured material — "coffee grounds" dominated by sheets of tree bark. The Spirit Lake peat at Mount St. Helens exhibits a textured slurry with flat bark sheets imbedded throughout, which greatly resembles Pennsylvanian coal beds and their vitrain bands. It also lies on the rather level lake bottom, with no significant highs or lows. It consists of over 90 percent organic material with some clay-size ash.

Rapid Fossilization

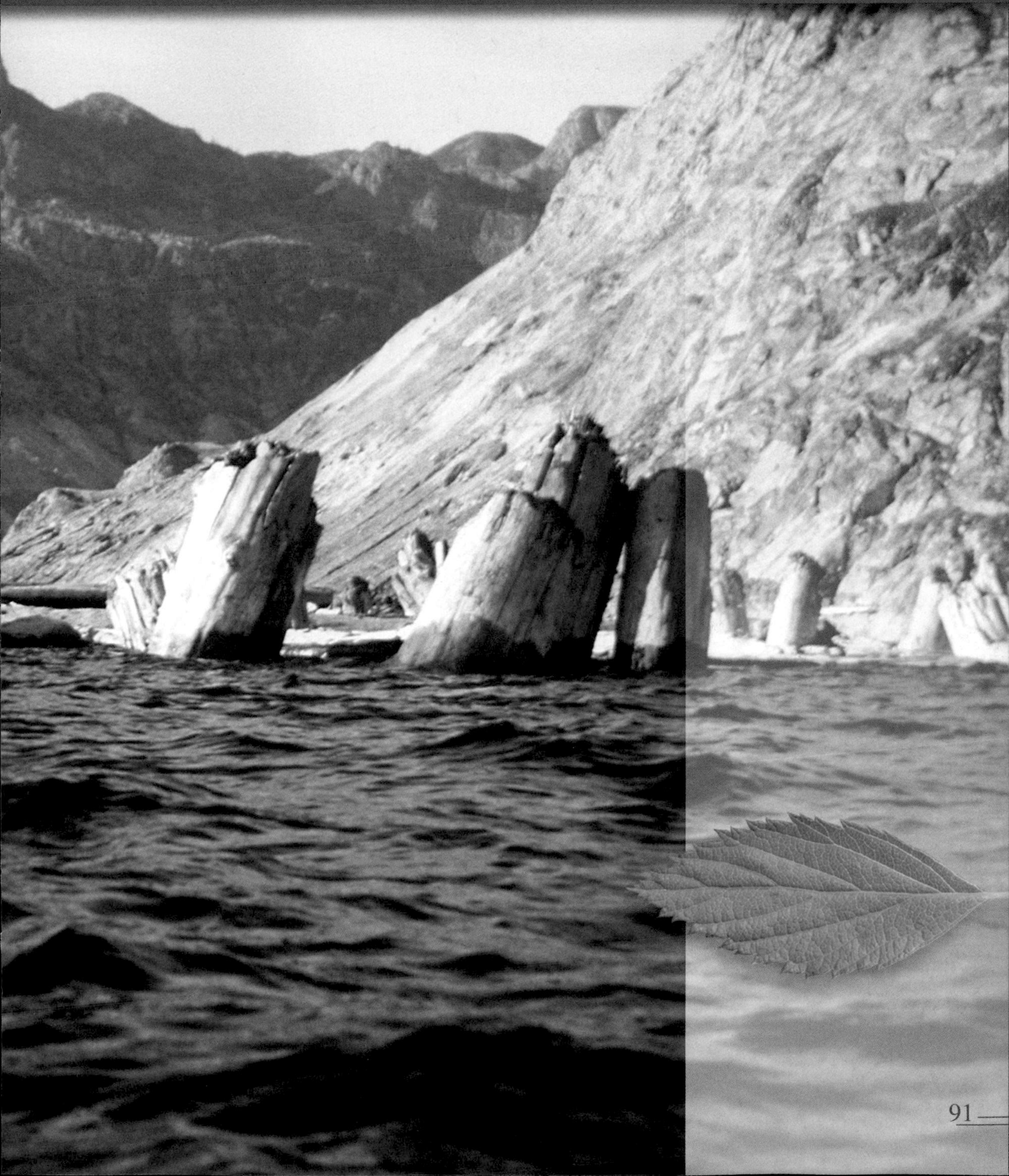

TREES IN PUMICE PLAIN

The avalanche and blast cloud transported and buried millions of trees. These were further buried by ash fall and subsequent mudflows. Most of the trees retained only their trunks, the root systems having been broken off and the branches stripped.

Because the burial causes were directional in nature, most of the logs were buried with a preferred orientation, pointing away from the volcano. As the blast cloud whipped down the slope and billowed among the hills, the trees were laid down in surrealistic swirls looking much like fingerprints. Erosion of the burial sites now exposes them. Petrifaction of wood and formation of fossils usually requires rapid burial in sediments deposited by moving fluids.

NAUTILOID FOSSILS IN GRAND CANYON

Investigating the proposed rapid deposition of the Redwall Limestone, creationist geologists discovered billions of large, well-preserved nautiloid fossils. These marine creatures were somewhat like a squid with a cigar-shaped shell

Redwall stand vertically within the bed arguing for very rapid burial of nautiloids and very quick halting of sediment around them. Fossil nautiloids confirm the underwater sediment flow hypothesis for the Redwall and refute the slow and gradual model proposed by uniformitarians. The pyroclastic flows at Mount St. Helens, being fast, high density slurry flows, help us understand how the nautiloids of the Grand Canyon were buried.

about the length of your arm. These abundant fossils occur within a single, 7 foot (2 meters) thick layer within the Redwall Limestone. The fossils lie oriented within a preferred direction in a deposit covering a large part of Arizona and Nevada. About 15 percent of nautiloids in the

Petrifaction is a special case of fossilization. For most fossils, the organic material is replaced by dissolved minerals in the ground water or host rock, allowing the fossil to retain the shape of the tree or organism but none of the organic material. Sometimes the replacing mineral is calcite, most often found in limestone. In petrified wood, the invader is usually silica, the primary constituent of sandstone. The ideal environment in which wood can be petrified is burial by volcanic ash, which is always full of silica.

Two families of processes might petrify wood. The most common is when the wood is buried deeply under great pressures by hot volcanic ash that contains abundant silica. Hot water dissolves the silica and the pressures inject it into the wood. The silica surrounds each woody cell, halting all organic activity.

The other common petrifaction process is when the individual molecules in the wood decay and are carried away by the ground water. This leaves a tiny molecule-size cavity behind. Into that cavity, a molecule of silica crystallizes. This process eventually replaces the entire piece of wood and can preserve intricate detail such as tree rings.

Petrifaction was once thought to require a long period of time, but it is often observed to happen rapidly. It can be accomplished in a laboratory simply by injecting silica into the wood. Wood has been observed to petrify rapidly at the hot springs at Yellowstone.

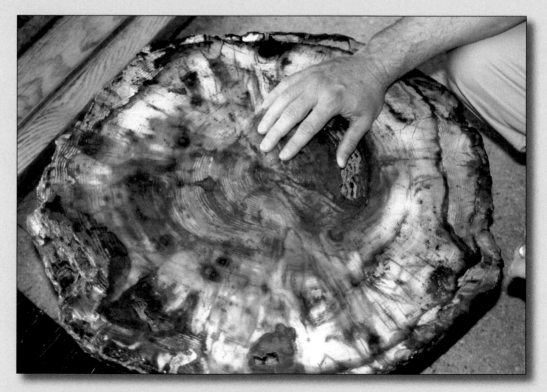

Ginkgo Petrified Wood showing rings

Trees in Arizona's Petrified Forest are typically oriented parallel to each other.

PETRIFIED FOREST IN ARIZONA

Deposits of buried trees are found in several places around the world. The most famous is the Petrified Forest in Arizona. It has long been interpreted as a once-standing forest, buried by a volcanic eruption and petrified in volcanic ash. The question is, "Was this a forest growing in place or did the forest grow some place else?"

Tree trunks by the thousands have been discovered here, often in pristine condition with no evidence of time for decay. Studies have revealed that the tree trunks, almost none of which are in an upright position, show a preferred orientation, with their long axis pointed in the same direction as if deposited by flowing mud. Branches are almost always stripped off, but the bark is often intact. More recent researchers have labeled this spectacular deposit as a "petrified log jam" transported in from the east, which implies that it is not a "petrified forest" at all.

At Mount St. Helens, many of the trees ripped from the ground by the water wave, blast cloud, and the mudflows eventually made their way into Spirit Lake. Though some were merely snapped in two, others were pulled out of the ground with a root ball at their base. Typically, they floated horizontally on the waters once things settled down.

Over the months, many of them began to turn and float upright with their roots down. In

and thus the trees tended to waterlog root end first. This tendency was similar to that observed among the trees carried down through the drainage basin by the mudflows — with roots down and trunks up and in growth position, but not growth location.

Over the years, the number of logs floating on the lake's surface has decreased, and it is presumed that they have settled to the bottom, with many still in their upright position. During the first twenty years after the 1980 eruptions, more than a half million logs were deposited on the floor of Spirit Lake. Because the lake actively receives sediment today, these upright trees on the bottom are being buried on the bottom as they grew, but not where they grew.

When the Army Corps of Engineers lowered the lake's original, dangerously high level, many logs lay on the new shoreline. Others had already waterlogged, had sunk in upright orientation to the bottom, and had been buried in the lake bottom sediments. The trunk pictured below was buried so deeply in those sediments that it remained upright even after the lake had been lowered. It did not grow here.

Upright floating logs

some, rocks were still present in the root balls, which further inclined the trunks to sink roots first. Furthermore, the natural system through which water is drawn into the tree is through the roots,

Upright trunk on the bank

The more interesting question was whether or not trees on the lake's bottom were still in upright position. In the days immediately following the eruption, the lake was so full of particulates that visibility was impossible, even to a scuba diver. Use of a "side-scanning sonar" device enabled researchers on the surface of the lake to ascertain the orientation of tree trunks that had already waterlogged and sunk.

The sonar printout shows sonar reflectors (dark) standing in vertical orientation above the lake bed with distinct sonar shadows (white) cast long distance over the flat surface.

Just five years after the main eruption, it was estimated from the sonar survey that over 20,000 logs had sunk to the bottom with their root ends buried in lake bottom sediments. If the lake were to be completely drained, it might look like a drowned forest, but these trees did not grow there. They grew on the nearby hillsides and were brought to this location by catastrophic processes. Remember, the bottom of the lake is now higher than the top of the lake was previously.

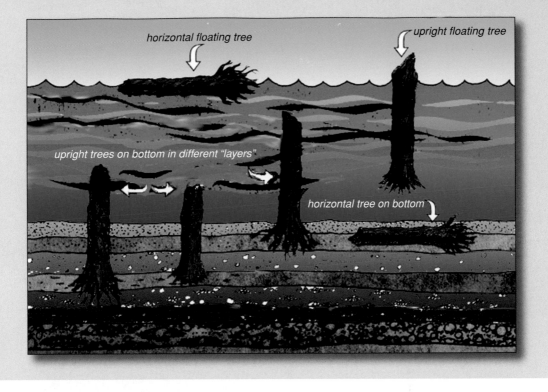

horizontal floating tree

upright floating tree

upright trees on bottom in different "layers"

horizontal tree on bottom

TREES IN SPIRIT LAKE

Volcanic events continued over several years, and sedimentation is continuing at a rapid pace to this day. Thus the sunken trees would have been and are still being buried or grounded in several layers. Logs from each species of tree sink at their own rate. Noble fir and Silver fir do not float as long as Douglas fir. Differing sink rates mean that one species ends up in one layer and then another species of upright trees sits in the overlying layer.

Suppose that over time the lake entirely fills in and the trees petrify. Then suppose that erosion exposes the upright petrified trunks with their roots in several layers. The series of tree-bearing sediments might be interpreted as a series of successive standing forests, each with a dominant species of tree and each buried by separate volcanic events many years apart. It might even be concluded that the entire series took over tens of thousands of years to develop; but it would be incorrect. These trees were all from the same forest. Different species grew side-by-side, were killed at the same time, and were transported together but got buried at slightly different times within different layers.

Tree rings record whether or not a growth year has been wet or dry or if there has been insect infestation, fire, or other forest-wide event. Comparing the tree rings from trunks gathered from several of these Spirit Lake layers would show that they all lived at the same time, even though buried in different "geologic layers." A similar series of layers has been discovered and studied in Yellowstone National Park.

CROSS-SECTION AT YELLOWSTONE PARK

One of the most famous petrified forests is to be found on the northeast corner of Yellowstone National Park. Here, a series of twenty-seven layers, each containing beautiful petrified trees in both upright and horizontal positions, lie exposed by erosion at Specimen Ridge. Over fifty such layers are found at nearby Specimen Creek.

This series has traditionally been interpreted as a series of consecutive forests, each requiring hundreds of years to grow before being buried by separate volcanic eruptions. The entire sequence must have taken, so it is thought by standard geologists, many tens of thousands of years to be deposited. Petrifaction followed and then erosion of the whole stack of layers exposed a cliff.

This site and its long-age interpretation has been one of the most effective arguments which purport to show that the earth is older than biblical chronology will allow. It has convinced many that the Bible cannot be trusted and thus can be disregarded.

PETRIFIED TREES

Yellowstone Park is famous for its abundance of hot, silica-rich waters. A major part of the park is actually an absolutely huge exploded and collapsed volcano which is still active as seen in geysers, mud pots, and other geologic phenomena. The environment for petrifaction is ideal. Trees growing near hot springs utilize the silica-rich water. They use the water, but the silica halts life functions. Sometimes the trees die by petrifaction.

Recent studies of the trees and deposits at Specimen Ridge have revealed a wide variety of evidence seemingly incompatible with the burial-in-place hypothesis. The logs, branches and twigs are oriented with their axes in a preferred direction, indicating movement by a fluid. Furthermore, the fossilized matter comes from more than one habitat. Some are from valley regions and others come from the mountains, yet each layer is now flat-lying.

PETRIFIED TREE SHOWING BEDDING

Every petrified tree, horizontal or vertical, shows which end was the root end and trunk and root ball have been snapped off at or near the ground level, no doubt leaving the bulk of the roots where the tree originally grew.

Each tree is encased in layers of sediment which show distinct bedding, the kind produced by flowing water or mud. Logs do not appear to be rooted in soil.

One might conclude that the trees grew somewhere else

for many a root ball remains. None of the petrified trees at Yellowstone, whether upright or horizontal, possess complete root systems. The and were rafted here by mudflows. Many may be in growth position, but none is in growth location.

MATCHING TREE RINGS FROM DIFFERENT LAYERS

The tree rings of trees found in several consecutive layers at Yellowstone Park were compared. If the trees lived at different times, their tree rings would show entirely different yearly patterns. If the trees lived at the same time and died in the same catastrophic volcanic event, they would retain similar patterns in their tree rings since they lived at the same time. They

would record the same history of environment throughout their lives, even if they were eventually buried in different layers.

A recent study of Yellowstone petrified wood did indeed find that the trees retained matching signature patterns in the tree rings. Thus, they lived at the same time and were transported and deposited within different strata by successive mudflows. They did not live in successive forests. This explains the accumulation of material from various habitats and the preferred orientation of the debris. When the flowing muds came to a halt, some of the trees had maintained their erect posture. The scenario seems quite similar to the rafting of the stumps by mudflows at Mount St. Helens and analogous to the sinking of trees in Spirit Lake.

YELLOWSTONE ROAD MARKERS

Visitors to the Yellowstone petrified "forest" in years past were greeted by an interpretive marker explaining a multi-thousand year scenario. When confronted with the evidence from Mount St. Helens, the interpreters removed the sign at Specimen Ridge and changed the sign at another upright petrified tree stump location to indicate that the trunk had been relocated by moving muds similar to those at Mount St. Helens.

It seems that one of the standard proofs that the Bible could not be trusted was itself in error, and the Bible still stands!

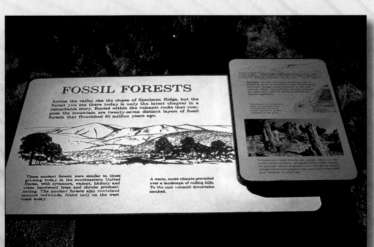

FOSSIL FORESTS

Across the valley rise the slopes of Specimen Ridge, but the forest you see there today is only the latest chapter in a remarkable story. Buried within the volcanic rocks that compose the mountain are twenty-seven distinct layers of fossil forests that flourished 50 million years ago.

These ancient forests were similar to those growing today in the southeastern United States, with sycamore, walnut, hickory and other hardwood trees and shrubs predominating. The ancient forests also contained sequoia redwoods, found only on the west coast today.

A warm, moist climate prevailed over a landscape of rolling hills. In the east volcanic mountains smoked.

RAPID REVEGETATION

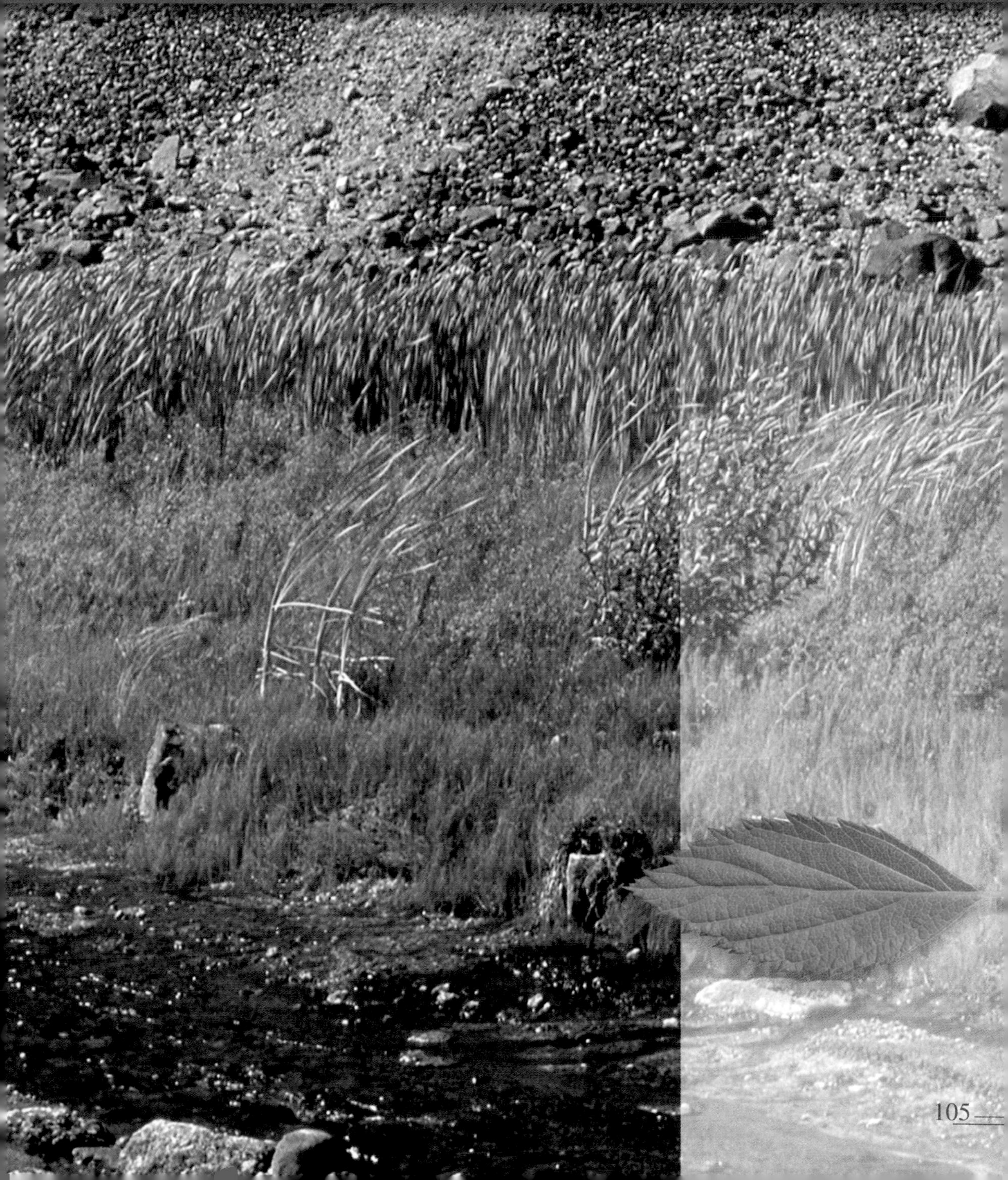

Biologists have been amazed at how quickly vegetation reappeared on the devastated slopes. Early predictions had claimed it would be over one hundred years before life could re-establish itself in the poisonous ash which covered everything. Despite the predictions, in just a few years, rain and snowfall have both broken down the ash into nutrients and resurrected the buried soil beneath, allowing plants to reappear in abundance.

In some cases, it appears that buried seeds and roots have re-germinated; in other circumstances, seeds or spores have blown in on the wind or been carried in by birds and insects. Plants new to the area have also found a home here. Many hillsides are actually green in the summer.

Perhaps even more startling is the rapid adaptation of certain animals to the new conditions. Some burrowing animals like pocket gophers survived the blast by being underground. Their predators on the surface were destroyed and, while food may have been scarce at first, they now seem to be thriving. There is even some worry of an overpopulation of the gophers. Other animals invaded the zone, taking advantage of the lack of competition for food.

Meanwhile large elk herds have returned and enjoy munching on the abundant sprigs that are sprouting in various places. Their scat enriches the soil and brings in more seeds. Other animals migrate in and out.

In the lake, strange algae pods soon flourished, but the fish seemingly did not survive. Now, however, a new ecology is establishing itself. Some fish have reappeared. A rather remarkable tailed frog lives in abundance in nearby pools of water.

God has designed His creation in such a way that it can adapt to a variety of conditions. Even though natural disasters take a toll, life persists and even thrives.

We normally think of elk as a forest-dwelling animal. Scientists were wondering how elk could survive in the unshaded blast zone.

Would their thick hides cause the animals to overheat in the summer? Scientists discovered that elk have a cooling behavior. They simply lie down in wet soil during hot summer afternoons. These animals easily adapt to the blast zone.

Today, an elk cow will give birth to one calf every two or three years; but, immediately after

the eruption, mother elk were witnessed bearing twins or triplets each year. Thus, the herd rapidly filled the "unfilled ecological niche."

Consider the days immediately following the Genesis Flood when the few survivors of each "kind" disembarked their refuge on the ark. They ventured into a world of wide open spaces, few competitors for food, and few predators. As they migrated away from the ark, they adapted to a variety of new conditions all the while multiplying rapidly. Their Creator had commanded them to "breed abundantly in the earth, and be fruitful, and multiply" (Genesis 8:17). At Mount St. Helens, we learn that their Creator had placed within them the physiological ability to obey His command.

EVIDENCES FOR CATASTROPHISM AT MOUNT ST. HELENS

1) Quickly Formed Stratification

Glowing "rivers" of volcanic ash moved at speeds up to 100 miles per hour (161 kilometers per hour). Thin layered strata were deposited. These resemble strata which might be supposed to require many thousands, even millions of years, to form.

2) RAPIDLY ERODED CANYONS

Canyons were eroded through solid rock. A new system of canyons forms the upper drainage basin of the North Fork of the Toutle River. It might seem that slow erosion formed these during countless thousands of years.

3) UPRIGHT DEPOSITED LOGS IN SPIRIT LAKE

Tens of thousands of logs, eroded from slopes around Spirit Lake, have been "replanted" in standing position on the bottom of the lake. These might seem to be a succession of forests grown during many thousands of years.

4) RAPIDLY FORMED PEAT LAYER IN SPIRIT LAKE

Sheets of conifer bark have accumulated in the lake as layered, coarse, textured peat. The deposit has significant similarity to the composition and texture of coal. Coal is usually assumed to be a slowly formed swamp deposit.

5) QUICK RECOVERY OF ECOSYSTEM IN BLAST ZONE

Living things survived in the most severely devastated areas and are flourishing in the adverse conditions. The extraordinary response of living things to catastrophe has caused textbooks on ecosystem recovery to be rewritten.

We Are Not in Control

Those of us who watched Mount St. Helens learned some important lessons. During the nine-hour eruption of May 18, 1980, the volcano released the energy equivalent to 440 million tons of TNT. That amount of power staggers our minds. We were powerless in changing the course of events that day. Yet, that eruption was only a small display of volcanic power. Imagine the colossal power released by the last big prehistoric explosion at Yellowstone – more than 2,000 times the energy of May 18. While thinking about volcanic power, we comprehend that we are not in control of our environment, our life, or our destiny. Someone else is in control. An impersonal force resident within matter and energy does not control the cosmos.

The Bible tells us that a personal, transcendent God is in control. The Psalmist exclaimed, "He touches the mountains and they smoke" (Psalm 104:32). A miniscule amount of God's power was on display at Mount St. Helens that day. We witnessed just God's "little finger" in operation. The Bible tells us that the hands of God were on display during the third day of creation week as the continents were being shaped (Psalm 95:5). It took the entire outstretched arm of God to fashion the universe (Jeremiah 32:17). We stand in awe of the power of the creator, and sustainer God.

The Future Seems Uncertain

While researching the slopes of Mount St. Helens, we experienced a sense of uncertainty. While we were working on the mountain, we were mindful that the volcano could explode at any time. We were looking for signs that might indicate the degree of danger near the volcano. We remembered Harry Truman (not the U.S. president) who at 80 years old had lived a major part of his life at his lodge on the south shore of Spirit Lake just north of the volcano. Harry refused to heed the warning signs. He died on May 18.

We also thought about those people who lived in the days just before the great flood of Noah's day. They did not heed the warning signs and refused the ark of safety that God offered to Noah and his family. The primary purpose of Noah's flood was one of judgment. The Bible tells us that civilization before the Flood was incredibly wicked (Genesis 6:5-13), and it has always been true that "the wages of sin is death" (Romans 6:23). Total destruction of all life was not God's intention, however, so Noah was instructed to build the ark on which his own believing family could be saved, along with representatives of the land-dwelling, air-breathing animals. God "brought" those chosen animals to Noah, perhaps by instilling in the chosen pairs the ability to sense impending danger and migrate to safety.

We also thought of our generation and the judgment day that the Lord's justice requires. The Bible says, "He has appointed a day on which He will judge the world in righteousness by the Man whom He has ordained. He has given assurance of this to all by raising Him from the dead" (Acts 17:31). We wonder when God will intervene again in human affairs.

Harry Truman died May 18, 1980.

WE NEED TO THINK IN A DIFFERENT DIMENSION

We have learned from Mount St. Helens that our experience with the earth limits our reasoning ability. On the surface, "uniformity" appears an elegant way to reason about the earth processes. Harry Truman had no experience with an exploding volcano. He staked his life on his belief in "uniformity," and he died during the catastrophe. Ideas about catastrophes are shackled by the fact that we live in a "uniformitarian" world that is dominated by uniform processes. When a catastrophe does occur, like the eruption of Mount St. Helens, a veil is lifted from our mind's eye, and we can comprehend, to a greater degree, the much more intense processes that could have shaped the earth. At the volcano we get a glimpse of the way Noah's flood must have been.

Two basic ways exist for interpreting geologic deposits. The traditional view, represented by the slogan "the present is the key to the past," assumes that processes have operated throughout the past in much the same fashion as they do today. This view, called the "principle of uniformity," relies heavily on slow and gradual processes interspersed with sporadic minor catastrophes, such as happen today.

The second view, currently gaining favor among geologists, holds that there have been episodes in earth history dramatically different from anything observed today. Much emphasis is placed on major storms, floods, volcanic eruptions, asteroid bombardment, and similar catastrophes, far greater in scope than anything witnessed by modern observers.

The Bible speaks of a great water cataclysm in the days of Noah, which accomplished extensive geologic work. Modern processes such as rainfall, erosion, deposition of sediments, fossilization, volcanism, and others, would have been operating at rates, scales, and intensities far beyond anything observed today. Noah's flood totally restructured the surface of the earth and laid down, among other things, many layers of sediment full of the remains of dead plants and animals. The sediments soon hardened into rock, and the organic material fossilized. We see those deposits now as sedimentary rocks and fossils. ___ ___ great amounts of volcanic ___ ___ck, far greater than could ___ ___day's conditions. These ___ ___en interpreted under ___ ___ity, are thought to provide e___ ___n and the old earth. That interpreta___ ___cludes the denial of both the Flood a___ ___

In the Bible, God pro___ ___ Noah and all of mankind that He would ne___ send another globally destructive flood. God has been true to His promise and no other event like the Flood has occurred since then. It is difficult therefore, for geologists who believe the Flood was geologically significant, to reconstruct the events that laid down the various geologic deposits, for we have no natural events to study today which are comparable in scale or circumstance.

The eruption at Mount St. Helens, however, does provide an analog for Noah's flood and helps us understand its nature. While the 1980 eruption was much smaller than many historic volcanic eruptions and trivial compared to many that occurred in the past, it was quite catastrophic on a local scale. Many of the components of the eruption were similar to those that must have operated during the flood.

Furthermore, the activity at Mount St. Helen's was well studied and documented, and, as such, it provides insight into the flood and helps us interpret Flood deposits. The use of Mount St. Helens' catastrophic eruption and the events surrounding it as an analog for Noah's flood becomes reasonable as we recognize that many of the events associated with the eruption were, in fact, water related. The rapid mudflows, the erosion, the wave on Spirit Lake, the log mat — all were processes likewise common during Noah's flood. Even the volcanic cloud that was ejected was 90 percent steam.

Mount St. Helens shows us how our old thinking pattern is deficient and challenges us to think in a different dimension. The Bible says, "...these times of ignorance God overlooked, but now commands all men everywhere to repent" (Acts 17:30). If we are honest with ourselves, we must agree that many times we fall far short of God's pattern for our lives. The Bible says "the wages of sin is death," but it also continues, "the gift of God is eternal life through Jesus Christ our Lord" (Romans 6:23). It also tells us how the wages were paid and the gift of eternal life made possible — for "Christ died for our sins" (I Corinthians 15:3). We are desperate sinners and deserve the penalty of death which He took upon Himself.

Noah's ark during the Global Flood

The rapid recovery of plants and animals at Mount St. Helens reminds us that life continues after catastrophe. We learned that plants and animals have amazing abilities to cope with very difficult conditions. Plants and animals can even flourish at locations and in circumstances that seem impossible. Elk migrated to safety before the eruption at Mount St. Helens, and animals migrated to Noah's ark in the days before the Flood. So we must come to God's present-day offer for salvation. One way or another, each of us will live for eternity.

Christ, who lived a sinless life and deserved no death penalty, agreed to pay our penalty by His death on the Cross, thereby providing eternal life and guaranteeing it by His Resurrection from the dead. In doing so, He gained victory over both sin and death for all eternity.

The New Testament explains that the ark of Noah has a lesson for us about Jesus Christ. Just as Noah and his family escaped the global, watery judgment of sin in their day by accepting God's provision of salvation in the Ark, so we can be saved from the global, fiery judgment of sin to come by accepting God's provision of salvation today. Jesus Christ is God's gracious provision to us. A Christian is one who has boarded the Ark, as it were. He has recognized his own sinful, helpless position before God as one deserving eternal death. However, he also recognizes that his sins have been paid for, that the penalty has been paid by a Substitute. Each individual must go before the Heavenly Father and ask Him to specifically apply Christ's death to his own sins, thereby gaining forgiveness. Doing so is the only way to escape the coming judgment and receive eternal life.

Physical evidence, such as seen at Mount St. Helens, can never substitute for faith, but it can point to the object of our faith and demonstrate the reasonableness of that faith. What we have seen encourages the Christian and answers many questions, showing that the biblical view of history and life is the most valid. It removes doubts that may have kept an individual from believing. It also confronts the skeptic with evidence that was observed by a host of careful observers. This evidence of geological processes and results supports God's Word when it claims that God created all things in the not-too-distant past. The original creation was "very good" (Genesis 1:31). Creation was ruined by Adam's rebellion, for the penalty of sin is death. Creation was judged and the world restructured by the global flood of Noah's day, but it was redeemed through the death of Christ.

Our response must be to change our minds and adopt correct thinking in all areas from science to daily life. If we do so, the lessons that we learned at Mount St. Helens can last for eternity.

As president of the Institute for Creation Research (ICR) in California, and a widely respected author in his own right, Dr. John Morris brings an impressive combination of scientific knowledge and uncompromising faith to his work. With his Ph.D. in Geological Engineering, he has authored a number of articles, publications, and books — including those on geology and the biblical truths of creation. Titles include *The Young Earth* and *Is the Big Bang Biblical?* He is also the co-author of *The Modern Creation Trilogy.*

Dr. Steven Austin received his doctorate in geology from Pennsylvania State University. He is currently the chairman of the Geology Department at the Institute for Creation Research in San Diego, California. His specialty is the sedimentary processes that form rock strata, fossils, and fossil fuels. While a student at the University of Washington before the 1980 eruptions, Dr. Austin walked on the slopes of Mount St. Helens seeking to understand the processes that formed the Earth. He has led 15 research expeditions to the Grand Canyon, written numerous research papers, and lectured widely on creation. *Footprints in the Ash* is his third published book.

PHOTO CREDITS